Resorts of Maldives

RESORTS OF MALDIVES

PICTURES, WORDS AND DESIGN
BY ADRIAN NEVILLE

2002

S

SEVEN HOLIDAYS

SevenHolidays
adrian@sevenholidays.com

First edition - 1998 (Novelty Printers and Publishers)
Second edition - 2002

ISBN: 955-8537-00-4

Copyright © Adrian Neville

Typeset in Journal (Emigre), ITC Oficina Sans and Adobe Myriad

about the two coloured boxes
'Relative Price' indicates the price of the
resort relative to the other resorts.
Number '1' indicates the most expensive
resort and number '10' indicates the
cheapest.

The **'Density of rooms to island size'**
indicates the number of rooms relative to
the size of the island. The higher the
number and the darker the colour, the
more rooms they have squeezed onto the
island.

Introduction

THE COUNTRY

location
In the Indian Ocean, an hour's flight southwest of Sri Lanka and southern India. The country is 820 kilometres in length stretching to just below the equator.

geography
An archipelago of around twenty six atolls of very varied size sustaining around 1,190 islands. Of these, 200 are inhabited and 90 are, or soon will be, resorts. All the islands are low lying. The highest point in the country is three metres but most islands are less than one and a half metres above sea level.

population
Around 280,000, of which some 80,000 live on Male', the capital. Everyone is Muslim (Sunni) and speaks Dhivehi, although the southern islands have a distinct dialect.

currency
Maldivian Rufiyaa. Tourists may do all their business in US Dollars. The exchange rate has long been fixed at 11.72 rufiyaa to one dollar. For a thousand years and more, the medium of exchange was the cowrie shell (cyprea moneta) which was farmed in the Maldives and taken from here all around the world.

climate
The temperature is constantly between 26°C - 30°C. Two distinct seasons divide the year. The North-East monsoon runs from December through to April. This is the tourist high season when there is little rainfall, wide blue skies and endless hours of sunlight. The South-West monsoon runs from May through to November. During this period it is still generally dry and sunny though there is sporadic rainfall and cloud cover (rarely prolonged enough to spoil a holiday). At the turn of the monsoon winds it is rough and rainy for a couple of weeks.

clothing
Informal, light cotton clothes are ideal. Any length of shorts, tops and swimwear is acceptable on the resort islands, but nudity is forbidden. Guests may wish to bring a set of smarter clothes for the evening. When taking a local island visit or a trip to Male' it is recommended, out of respect for Maldivian sensitivities, that longer, less informal, clothes are worn.

local time
GMT + 5 hours

business hours
7.30 - 14.30 in the government sector and from 9.00 - 23.00 for most shops.

ARRIVAL

airport

Just as every resort island is a single hotel, so Hulhule is nothing but the airport. It sits a short distance off the coast of Male' like a huge aircraft carrier at anchor. The following are the international airlines and charter flights currently flying in: Aeroflot, Air Europe, Air Holland, Air Madeira, SriLankan Airlines, Airtours International, Air 2000, Austrian Airlines, Balair, Balkan Airlines, Britannia, Condor, Cross Air, Emirates, Eurofly, Indian Airlines, Lauda Air, LTU International Airlines, Malaysian Airlines, Monarch Airways, Pakistan International Airlines, Singapore Airlines.

customs & immigration

A full flight and a busy morning will mean several minutes queuing. The formalities themselves are straightforward. Everyone gets a free 30 day visitors' visa. If you have recently passed through a country in which contagious diseases have been reported, you may be asked to show a certificate of inoculation. There is nothing specific that you need for the Maldives. It is well worth noting here that malaria does not exist in the country. The following items are prohibited: alcohol, drugs, pornography and idols of worship. People caught with illegal drugs are particularly harshly dealt with. Other items will be confiscated and returned to the guest when he or she leaves.

no booking

There is no requirement to have your holiday already booked by the time you arrive in the country but my serious advice is don't turn up without a booking. The simple reason is you will pay far more for your holiday if you do. Travel agents and tour operators in your country pass on some of the discounts they receive from the resorts. Organising a holiday at the airport means you will probably pay the highest possible price. However, if you do find yourself at the airport without a paid-up holiday you can either go to the Tourism Ministry's Information counter, check out the many individual resort booths that are lined up outside the building or negotiate with some of the representatives of the local travel agents. There won't be any bargains.

transfers

Assuming you have a booking, you will be met outside the main building by representatives of your tour operator or resort. They will sort out your transfer to the resort itself. There are three ways of getting from the airport to your resort: by dhoni (local boat), by speedboat and by air. Obviously the distance to the resort dictates which modes of transport are feasible. The king of the transfers is a seaplane flight on a cloudless day. You are unlikely to see anything quite like it again. The largest of the seaplane transfer companies is called Maldives Air Taxi and they fly to each of the resorts that sport their banner advert in the following pages.

THE RESORTS

There are, at the present time, eighty nine resorts in the country. But there are always a few that are temporarily closed for renovations or major changes brought about by new owners or operators. This guidebook only shows those resorts that are open. As the new and renewed ones open up I will photograph and review them for inclusion in the next edition.

What's the difference?

It's amazing just how different one resort can be from another. To be honest, it's also amazing how just about everyone who comes to the Maldives has a great holiday no matter where they end up. But if you put some thought into what you definitely would like to have on your island and what you would rather not find there, then find it in this book, you're on your way to a truly memorable couple of weeks. Here is a list of the main things to consider as you surf for your ideal 'getaway':

Some islands have a policy of getting a good mix of nationalities but most resorts tend to have more of one nationality than any other. And a few resorts are all Italian. Even if you love the sound of a particular island, it may be a mistake to take your holiday there.

Although there is a dive base on every single resort and although there is no such thing as a bad place for diving in the country, some islands are much more focused on diving than others. If you are a keen diver these are the ones to seek out. There will be more frequent diving on offer, more options available (such as night diving, nitrox diving and all-day safaris) and more fellow divers to share your experiences with.

If you don't dive but you're a keen snorkeller then you want to find a resort that has a surrounding reef with at least some of it close to shore. It is at the drop-off that you'll find the variety and number of fish. If you are a beginner or nervous swimmer then any fair-sized lagoon will do for you. A really close reef drop-off wouldn't be ideal.

For learning watersports a large, deep lagoon is best. For watersport experts, find the few resorts that have large setups and active staff (I have tried to indicate in the book which these are).

For the sun worshipper, well, you can't miss. But do you like to have a lot of people around for the fun, games and evening activities or are you looking for a private spot and an early bed? The Maldives is great for both, but read up to make sure to don't make a terrible mistake.

A number of islands take just a few minutes to completely walk around, others are relatively huge. Some don't have much in the way of vegetation and coconut palms (but wonderful beaches), others have towering green interiors and picturesque palm trees leaning out over the water (but maybe unsightly groynes and sea walls).

The Maldives is one of the truly great holiday destinations of the world. The variety it offers under the sun and under the water will keep you coming back for years, checking out one resort after another looking to find that perfect paradise. If it is to be found anywhere on this earth, it might well be here, somewhere...

MALE'

They say there are two Maldives, Male' and the rest of the country. Any comparisons between the simple, quiet life of the islands and the competitive vigour of this pocket-sized capital city are becoming more and more tenuous with every passing year. Male' is the funnel through which almost all political, social and economic activity passes, trickling out to the 'fisherman's islands'. It is as rich, as modern and as forward thinking as anywhere in South Asia. A half-day visit will give you the flavour of the place and a chance to check out the historical highlights and do a bit of shopping.

Conveniently, everything you need to see is within a few minutes walk of the arrival jetty. The waterfront itself offers a pleasant stroll, a couple of restaurants, a square to rest in and look around, and the main market areas, including the not-to-be-missed fish market. Just behind the front are the historical sights: the fine modern mosque, the old Friday Mosque, the first presidential palace, the museum and Sultan Park. An informative guide is a great help in appreciating these places, but beware of those whose main aim is to steer you as quickly as possible to the shops where they get a commission. Touts are a bit of a pain now in Male' and you should not have any qualms about ignoring them.

Having said that, shopping is rewarding here. On the one hand, it is probably the most convenient places in South Asia to buy quality electronic goods, watches and cameras, while on the other hand, there's a good selection of tourist souvenirs worth haggling for. After a history here of at least eight hundred years the trade in turtle shell products is now illegal. Any that you see in the shops will be from old stock. The two largest souvenir specialists are Najaah Art Palace and Souvenirs. These are also friendly and trustworthy places worth singling out amongst the many.

DIVING

the dives

Almost every dive in the Maldives is a drift dive. This is a wonderful, effortless way of watching the underwater world pass by. With the current coming into the atoll bringing fresh, clean water the visibility might be fifty metres and the big pelagics might be queueing up to watch you pass by. But, on the other hand, there is an ever-present danger, however small, that a current will take you away from the atoll and out into into the deep blue. It is the job of the instructor (often with the help of an experienced boat captain) to assess the local conditions before any diver jumps in the water. It is a tribute to the professionalism of the dive centres that accidents have been extremely rare and life-enhancing dives an everyday occurence.

the coral

Few divers paid much attention to the corals when they went diving in the Maldives, fish was what they were looking for, particularly the big ones: whale sharks, sharks, mantas, turtles, napoleon wrasse, tunas...Then, in 1998, widespread coral bleaching occurred due to a too warm sea that moved around the Indian Ocean and suddenly people noticed the broken, grey stone walls where once, they remembered, there used to be colour. The fish numbers never decreased but some of the beauty of a dive had gone with the corals. Now the corals are back. And divers are not just looking at the fish but also checking out the coral regrowth. A field of young, pink soft coral swaying in the current is a new delight, so is the sight of pristine white juvenile hard corals and new coral breaking out of the cracks of an ancient brain coral. Brand new species to the Maldives are being discovered and identified.

the fish

There is a greater number of fish and a greater variety of fish in the Maldives than just about anywhere else in the world, Furthermore, there are laws and regulations in place that protect those fish and their environment. Most other dive regions have laws and regulations too but in the Maldives they are adhered to and that is not so common. The Maldives is also fortunate in not having to cope with the livelihood demands of a large and fast-increasing population. What we have here is a true diving paradise. Please do your bit to keep it that way.

dive centres

Every resort has its own dive centre. Almost across the board the equipment is new or nearly new, the brands are top-of-the-line and the maintenance is first class. You can be confident in hiring everything you need. If you prefer to bring your own wetsuit a half-size 3mm one is enough, unless you are going to do more than one dive a day. The water is consistently between 27°C and 30°C. Every dive centre offers open water certification and some form of introductory or discovery dive.

The areas where one dive centre differs from another is in service. I don't just mean loading and unloading the baskets from the boats and talking to the guests in the evening but also things like information and presentation of the local habitats, the number of divers per boat/instructor, the variety of dive sites on offer each day, the type of diving on offer (multi-dives, full-day, night diving, nitrox etc.) and the amount of effort put into learning and adjusting to new guests' standard and preferences. The dive company's web site is one place to start to find out what's on offer, then it's a matter of word of mouth and reputation.

ANGAGA

Flying.......30 mins
Speed boat.......n/a
Dhoni.......n/a

Ari Atoll, south

plentiful. The buildings are well designed and unobtrusive.

So why isn't it the perfect island? Because for several years it was not well maintained, nor well managed. There was a decline in facilities and service. But in 2000 the island was bought be the people who have Thulagiri and a gradual process of renovation is under way. In a couple of years it should be back among the best.

One of the best all-island beaches in the country.

As you approach the island, the only buildings visible are the twin roofs of the bar and restaurant. These are thatched and elegantly shaped like the upturned hulls of two dhonis. Under the high roof is a white sand floor, with comfy seats in the bar and plenty of space between tables in the restaurant (with extra space for honeymooners). The food is now good. Breakfast and lunch are buffet, dinner is set. All holidays are **full board**, though there is a small coffee shop for extra snacks. (It also offers an alternative lobster dinner).

There are 50 **rooms**, all the same, with hot and cold water, air conditioning and a fridge (buy your own drinks to put in). Each room has a traditional style swing on its large, shady verandah. The inside of the room is plain, the bathroom is partly open to the sky. All would be very well, except that when I visited the tap and

〰️ ANGAGA IS ONE OF THE BEST RESORTS - AT LEAST IN appearance. The wide open beaches go all the way around the island, unobstructed by bungalows, walls, groynes or thatched sun shades. The reef edge is very close by for two thirds of the island, and on the other third there is a large, gradually sloping, sandy bottomed lagoon. The palm trees are tall and

shower water was a mix of desalinated and salt water. This was a major disappointment, though I am now assured salt water is no longer used.

A major plus is the great beach outside every room. And just beyond that, good **snorkeling** and **diving** on the house reef. A short boat trip away is Angaga Thila (a column of coral). Here you will find an

exceptional number and variety of fish, including the grey reef shark. But apart from that, the renowned dive sites are much further away.

There is a full programme of excursions and fishing trips, though they are not well advertised. The evening entertainments are not set but vary from week to week according to the wishes or character of the guests.

Most of the guests are German speaking, though there are also a fair number of Italians, British and Australians. Despite its, hopefully temporary, decline in standards, the resort is often full. And the reasons why are obvious. It has an good, nearby reef that is recovering well, a varied lagoon and one of the best all-round-the-island beaches in the country.

Resort	*tel*: 450510	*fax:* 450520
	email:	
can of beer: $4.95		half day-
lime juice: $3.30		island hopping: $20
mineral water: $4.40		sunset fishing: $10
Dive centre		Divebase Angaga
	single dive, all equipment: $49	
	six dives, all equipment: $318	
	certified open water course: $465	

ARI BEACH

Flying.......16 mins
Speed boat.......180 mins
Dhoni.......n/a

Ari Atoll, south-east

The standard rooms are plain and simple, but they are newly refitted out and entirely satisfactory (a/c, telephone and waterjug, no hot water). The superior are similar but have a minibar, hot water shower and face the beach. The superior deluxe are unique A-framed buildings, like boat houses on inhabited islands. They are a little bigger, more private and have a better section of the beach. It is a sad, but seemingly inevitable, fact that here, as elsewhere, they have had to indulge in some lagoon sand pumping and unobtrusive groynes to keep what have always been long stretches of the finest white sand.

IT'S AN ODD FACT THAT AS YOU WALK FROM THE southern end to the northern end of this island you visibly progress up market. The suites of the new water bungalow village, on the northern tip, are over four times more expensive than the standard rooms found at the other end of the island. On the way you pass the superior and then the superior deluxe rooms.

In fact, the new water bungalow village, called Dhidhoo Finolhu, is marketed and sold as a separate resort. There is, though, completely free access between the two ends and, it's the bar area of Dhidhoo that is the happening place at night.

Ari Beach was one of the first resorts built in Ari Atoll and although it is starting to fray around the edges, it's still true to the original Maldives concept of keeping it simple and changing nature as little as possible. The local materials of coral, wood, woven palms and thatch are used very successfully, particularly in the delightful sunset-facing bar that doubles as an à la carte restaurant.

The rooms of Dhidhoo Finolhu Water Village are quite simply gorgeous. With its outward sloping walls it is shaped like some officer's room in a fine old galleon.

Relative price

10 6

7

Density of rooms to island size:

The interior design is a most tasteful mix of light pine boards and grainy, dark coconut palm, with white cotton textiles and a kilim for the floor. There are also three double-sized suites and even two unconnected honeymoon rooms, reachable only by boat.

The sundecks of the water bungalows are hidden from its neighbours. The lagoon here, though, is very shallow at low tide. The best swimming and watersports is to be had on the other side of the 'mainland', where there is plenty of beach and an outlet of the fully-stocked and unusually active Boomerang Watersports Centre. If watersports is among your priorities, then Ari Beach should be in your short list.

This is south-east Ari Atoll, so the diving is some of the best around, and although the dive centre is small it is surprisingly comprehensive. It not only has nitrox, but it is a five star instructor development centre.

Italians are the most numerous on Dhidhoo and the British are most numerous on Ari Beach. Germans come in second on both counts and French fourth. The old motto of 'no news, no shoes' still holds true for the mainland resort, but not for Dhidhoo.

A single island with two different resorts

Resort *tel*: 445367   *fax*: 445366
email: aribeach@dhivehinet.net.mv

can of beer: $2.65   half day-
lime juice: $1.60   island hopping: $20
mineral water: $4.25   sunset fishing: $20

Dive centre   EuroDivers
single dive, all equipment: $44
five dives, all equipment: $208
certified open water course: $337

Asdu Sun Island

Flying.....n/a
Speed boat.....95 mins
Dhoni.....n/a

North Malé Atoll

〜〜 THIS RESORT IS LIKE
A HIDDEN JEWEL. NEVER
advertised, and tucked inside the north
of North Malé Atoll, it is a sparkling
example of the 'original Maldives style'.

Essentially this means the minimum of
development. There are just thirty rooms
and a single reception, bar and restaurant building. There is no second restaurant or separate coffee shop, no satellite
tv or karaoke lounge, no swimming pool
and no tennis court.

Even the number of staff is kept to a
minimum. Many of the waiters go fishing,
everyone helps sweeping around in the
morning, and the barman knows all about
the reservations. It all works smoothly
under the genial eye of Ahmed Ismail and
his wife who own, run and live on the
resort.

The guests here tend to be a little older
than the average and often drawn from
the professions. A majority of the guests
are Italian, with Swiss and French making
up most of the rest. But, of course,
anyone who can fit in is most welcome.

Nouvelles Frontieres (Italy) take around
half of the rooms, the others Ahmed
Ismail fills, mostly by fax or e-mail, with
old friends, new friends or friends of
friends. It's that kind of place. The kind
of place where almost everyone goes to
the jetty to see their new-found friends
off. Or gets up for dawn with a group on
their last morning.

All the **rooms** are the same. They are
slightly higher and larger than most.
They have a telephone but no hot water
and no air conditioning. The latticed
space below the roof and the slatted
windows keep the sun out but let the
breeze through. It is a practical and
stylish design using local wood, coir rope
and screw-pine matting. All the rooms are
just a few metres from the water.

*There is a feeling of being all
alone in the middle of the
Indian Ocean*

Islands inside atolls tend to have smaller lagoons and better beaches than those on the outside, and this is no exception. There are several different **beaches** here divided by protruding bushes or the low coral groynes, giving the opportunity for privacy even on this small island. The **snorkelling** is excellent and the reef edge near-by.

The **dive** base is not very large nor very busy, but it is very well priced, and the diving in the region is first class, with a mix of local thilas and superb channel dives on the eastern edge of the atoll, above Meerufenfushi. There isn't much in the way of watersports here, but the kayaks are free and the windsurfers very cheap (or not even charged for).

Also refreshingly cheap are the drink prices (beer $2.65, lime juice $1.60 and bottles of wine from $10). And even the laundry is free. It is nice not to get stung for extras.

All the **meals** are set. It is not gourmet stuff, but it is good, tasty fare based around a lot of fresh fish caught that day (usually by your waiter or another member of staff).

From anywhere on Asdu there are just two islands visible on the horizon, the resort Meerufenfushi and the inhabited island Dhiffushi. There is a feeling of being all alone in the middle of the Indian Ocean. With its natural environment, simple style and peaceful atmosphere, Asdu has a magic that needs to be experienced to be understood.

Relative price.

Density of rooms to island size:

Resort	tel: 445051 fax: 440176
	email: info@asdu.com

can of beer: $2.65	half day-
lime juice: $1.60	island hopping: $15
mineral water: $4.25	sunset fishing: $15

Dive centre — Sub Maldive
single dive, all equipment: $52
six dives, all equipment: $302
certified open water course: $400

ATHURUGA

Flying.......25 mins
Speed boat.......n/a
Dhoni.......n/a

Ari Atoll, centre

Night fishing, island hopping and all the usual events and excursions (plus a few more) are changed each week, and clearly advertised in the reception.

Most unusually, there is no minimum number of passengers for excursions, so if a couple want a trip to a local island, it is set up for them ($15). This excellent individual service is noticeable across the board and comes from a thoughtful and responsive management.

Hard to beat such a value-for-money, quality resort

The food in the **restaurant** is outstanding, especially in the high season when the Italians demand it as a priority.

There are forty two identical **rooms**, all of the same high standard. Each one has a beach frontage, though it is not always wide (and there are a few old, low groynes interrupting it). The really good **beach** is on the main jetty side, in front of the theatre, bar and restaurant building (with its outside café).

The lagoon on this side is small, so the superb **house reef** is well within swimming distance. On the opposite side of the island the lagoon is very large and sandy, so it is ideal for paddling around in, and for children.

The **dive school**, called The Crab, looks as sparkling new as the rest of the place, and is equally well run. Here, Maldivian helpers do all the packing and carrying

~~ **ATHURUGA IS THE TWIN OF NEARBY THUDUFUSHI**; most things that are said about either are applicable to both. The first thing to say is that they are top class resorts.

The next thing to say is that the holidays here are **all-inclusive**. This increasingly popular option means different things on different islands, some clearly less inclusive than others. Here it means all drinks are free (you've already paid for them), except whisky and champagne; any amount, any time. One picnic, one island hop and one sunset fishing are also included. Snorkel and masks are free, as are the use of the canoes, windsurfers and catamarans. Water-skiing and big game fishing are available but not included.

In the high season there are many Italians here, with a number of Germans and British. For the rest of the year German speakers are in the majority, with British also in significant numbers. There are no complaints, as it is difficult to fault the running of the place.

Although the resort is seven years old it always looks like it has just been finished, such is the level and regularity of the maintenance. The buildings have a substantial feel to them, constructed of solid wood and coral stone. The public buildings are large and spacious and include a 'theatre' and dance floor where each night an amateur cabaret is put on by the staff.

Relative price:

5

8

Density of
rooms to
island size:

for you, as well as the washing and hanging up afterwards. As an island in the middle of the atoll, there is a longish boat ride to the outside channels, but there is compensation with one of the best thila dives in the atoll nearby. Around Atabu Thila (a large column of coral) you have the chance to swim with the swift and powerful dog-toothed tuna and the grey reef shark.

Overall the island sometimes has a 'built' feel, that is to say there is a large number of substantial buildings squeezing the space on a small island. But if this doesn't bother you (nor the piped music) then you would be hard pressed to beat such a value-for-money, quality resort.

| **Resort** | *tel*: 450508 | *fax*: 450574 |
| *email*: | | |

can of beer: incl.	half day-
lime juice: incl.	island hopping: $15
mineral water: incl.	sunset fishing: $15

Dive centre   The Crab
single dive, all equipment: $55
six dives, all equipment: $300
certified open water course: $480

BANDOS

Flying.....n/a
Speed boat.....20 mins
Dhoni.....n/a

North Malé Atoll

BANDOS IS ONE OF THE LARGEST AND OLDEST RESORTS

in the Maldives. At the heart of its continuing success is the combination of the relaxed, informal atmosphere of a typical Maldivian resort, with all the facilities and services that a large island close to Malé and the airport is expected to have.

Those facilities range from a conference centre to a swimming pool and as wide a *range of sports* as on offer anywhere. In the middle of the island, the sports centre provides squash, badminton, tennis, snooker, table tennis, darts, table football, a gym and an aerobics room. If just reading that makes you ache, they also provide a sauna, a steam room and massages to ease it all away.

The main reason for coming on holiday, for most people, is to be *in*active, so

those facilities are not heavily used. But one service offered at the centre is very welcome to parents. Qualified nannies are on hand to entertain children in the indoor and outdoor play areas. They baby sit as well, in the evenings.

The island overall is very good for *children*, with so much to do and so many other children around (relative to other islands). There is also a well-equipped medical centre with a doctor on call day and night.

Even after twenty six years of snorkelling and diving the *house reef* is still good. It is always within swimming distance of your door and still has a great abundance and variety of fish, though the run-off from rebuilding in the last couple of years has taken its toll.

One building that was rebuilt is the dive school which is now one of the biggest and most modern facilities in the country. It has one of the only

Relative price:

6

6

Density of
rooms to
island size:

decompresssion chambers. The dive sites are mostly to the east, on the outside of the atoll, where they are shared with the boats of the other resorts in this busy region. Although the sites are often dived, they are still in good condition and with in-going currents divers have excellent visibility of, among many others, tunas and barracudas, snappers and sharks. During the south-west monsoon season mantas regularly visit.

An informal,
cosmopolitan resort, on a
grand scale.

The **beach** goes all around Bandos, but it is never very wide. However,the minimal use of groynes and lack of sea walls make this more than acceptable. The narrowness is also partly due to the fact that the island has a good growth of trees, shrubs and bushes, that give much welcome shade.

The recent renovations included significant landscaping and a new walkway around the island,which has really improved the place.

Most of the one hundred and seventy five standard rooms have also been refurbished. Of the other fifty rooms, forty two are junior suites and eight are suites. Suites mean an extra sitting space added on to the front. Decorated in a rich style, they are a good size and have all the facilities one could expect, including minibar, phone and television.

In the evening the sand bar, situated between the beach and the coffee shop and restaurants, is a natural focus. With its low, cushioned wicker seats on the sandy floor and coconut wood columns, it is a comfortable, well serviced bar - particularly lovely when looking out to sea on moonlit nights. There is a dance floor at one end with regular discos and good live band performances.

The other buildings are necessarily large

though the specialist steak and sea food Harbour Grill is intimate in the evening, with outside seating overlooking the lagoon. The food in the main restaurant (again, completely renovated) is tasty and plentiful. At any time of day the coffee shop serves a wide selection of dishes, not always quickly.

Just about every nationality that holidays in the Maldives is represented here. This gives the place a cosmopolitan air. It is an informal resort on a grand scale.

Resort	tel: 440088	fax: 443877

email: bandos@dhivehinet.net.mv

can of beer: $3.85	half day-	speed b.
lime juice: $3.85	island hopping: $33	
mineral water: $3.00	sunset fishing: $22	

Dive centre   Dive Bandos
single dive, all equipment: $42
five dives, all equipment: $200
certified open water course: $440

BANYAN TREE

Flying.....n/a
Speed boat.....25 mins
Dhoni.....60 mins

North Malé Atoll

At the heart of the island is **the spa**. Enclosed in a tranquil hideaway, with incense and tinkling music in the air, guests give themselves up into the hands of expert Thai masseuses. The difficult part may be choosing from the list of seven different massages and nineteen other body, facial and beauty treatments. Prices are from $10 to $45.

The island's philosophy is summed up in their motto: a sanctuary for the senses

If the spa represents the senses of touch and smell, the sense of taste is well catered for too. The holidays here are full board, and few anyway would wish to miss out on the great lunch buffet, spread outside beneath the palms. Dinners are even better. Served at the table, with a selection for each course, they are **haute cuisine** on a desert island. Some of the best in the country.

In the evening the entertainment is of a **quiet** nature. There is no disco or karaoke here, and if you're looking for late night singing and drinking this isn't really the place. The large, open-sided bar overlooking the lagoon offers a satellite television room and a screen for movie projection, most often underwater films. It also has snooker, darts, board games and a small library. The shop attached must also go down as entertainment as it is the chicest and best stocked shop of any resort.

ᔕᔕ **BANYAN TREE HOTELS AND RESORTS ARE A NEW** company expanding quickly in the niche of fine small hotels of the world. This Banyan Tree, on the island of Vabbinfaru, opened in 1995 and immediately slotted into the very top echelon of resorts.

Everything expected of a five star resort is here, but what sets this place apart is the company's driving philosophy, summed up in the phrase "a sanctuary for the senses". It's all about calm and regeneration. And their techniques are essentially Asian.

During the day all the expected **sports** and entertainments are available, plus a couple of unexpected ones, and a number of them are free. Night fishing is free, so is sailing, catamaraning, wind-surfing, canoeing and the beach games. Water-skiing and deep sea fishing are available, and so is a moonlit dinner on a glass-bottomed boat.

The handsome *dive centre* has all new equipment and is run by a professional underwater photographer who offers services such as personalising his videos for you. Being inside the atoll the best dive sites are not nearby, but not too far either. Half the house reef is somewhat degraded, but the other half is excellent, with overhangs, sharks, lobster, rays and many other fish. The next door island, Ihuru, also has a fine house reef for snorkelling and diving.

Apart from some erosion in the northeast corner (where sandbagging, outer walls and groynes have been used) the *beaches* are very good, and the sand is particularly white and fine grained. This sand is spread over the floor of all the public areas and the paths that meander through the island, giving the place a smart but casual feel.

That smart but casual look is reflected in the architecture which is tremendously stylish but blends in perfectly with the environment. All the buildings are, in fact, Indonesian. Every piece of thatch and twining was imported from there.

The individual *villas* are particularly attractive and luxurious. The choice is between garden villas and beach villas. Some of each category have a jacuzzi as well. And there is one presidential suite.

Perhaps the only criticism that can be levelled at this resort is that there are perhaps too many villas for such a small, five star island. On all other counts, it's a dream of a place.

Relative price:

2

7

Density of rooms to island size:

Resort	tel: 443147	fax: 443843

email: reservations@banyantree.com.mv

can of beer: $4.50	half day-
lime juice: $4.50	island hopping: $25
mineral water: $2.50	sunset fishing: free

Dive centre   Banyan Tree Dive Centre
single dive, all equipment: $55
six dives, all equipment: $300
certified open water course: $545

Baros

Flying.....n/a
Speed boat.....20 mins
Dhoni.....50 mins

North Malé Atoll

∼∼ Baros IS A PRETTY RESORT WITH A LIVELY

atmosphere. In recent years it has been moving up market. The gardening, the rooms and the restaurants are now excellent and the service details are all in place.

There are seventy five **rooms**, sixteen of which are water bungalows, and all are handsome and well built. Constructed of dark wood, panels of woven screw pine and thatched roofs, they merge with their surroundings. They are also well serviced. Towels are changed constantly, and, while guests are in the restaurant, the rooms are tidied up, the bedsheets turned down and the lighting adjusted.

Calm during the day, the place livens up in the **evening**. The large Captain's Bar is next door to the equally large dance floor where, four nights a week, a live band plays and the good times roll until the early hours.

Nearly everyone here is on half board though bed and breakfast and full board are catered for. The coffee shop serves a comprehensive menu throughout the day and then, in the evening, alternates between a steakhouse, a barbecue buffet and à la carte restaurant. As well as this, and the main restaurant, is a smaller speciality restaurant serving buffets of different national food each night.

All the facilities of a large hotel, in an attractive, intimate setting

One face of the coffee shop looks west and draws a crowd at sunset to watch the sun go down and witness the feeding of rays in the shallows. The lagoon on this side, the jetty side, is large and sandy-bottomed (the right place for the watersports centre). On the other two thirds of the island it is small, with coral

Relative price:

6

9

Density of
rooms to
island size:

outcrops coming close to shore, so the snorkelling is excellent within the lagoon and at the reef edge.

The only disappointment is that there is an outer seawall built all the way around

this section of the island. The best that can be said about this is that after a while you tend not to notice it. Its function is to keep the beach in its place all year round and so far it has succeeded, as the **beach** is good to very good and almost uninterrupted.

Overall, the mostly German and British who come here are delighted with their choice. At a fair price you get the look and feel of a good hotel. The abundance

of flowers, the courteous service and the friendly atmosphere add up to a fun and pampered couple of weeks.

Resort	tel: 442672	fax: 443497
	email: sales@unisurf.com	

can of beer: $4.40	half day-
lime juice: $4.40	island hopping: $30
mineral water: $4.40	sunset fishing: $17

Dive centre   Baros
single dive, all equipment: $42
six dives, all equipment: $227
certified open water course: $406

BATHALA

Flying.......20 mins
Speed boat.......n/a
Dhoni.......n/a

Ari Atoll, north-east

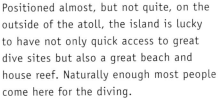

Maldives", and Fish Head, described as "the grey reef shark capital of the Maldives". The latter has also been called one of the ten best dive sites in the world!

BATHALA IS A CHEAP, SMALL AND VERY ATTRACTIVE

island. It is also, like its neighbours, a *dive island*.

Positioned almost, but not quite, on the outside of the atoll, the island is lucky to have not only quick access to great dive sites but also a great beach and house reef. Naturally enough most people come here for the diving.

The four resorts of Bathala, Maayafushi, Ellaidhoo and Halaveli have the whole of the north-east of Ari Atoll to themselves. On the inside of the atoll are two famous thilas (now Protected Marine Areas) : Maaya Thila, which has been described as "the white tip reef shark capital of the

On the outside of the atoll are any number of enticing channel dives and several more top class thila dives. The list of resident fish includes barracuda, turtle, tuna, eagle ray, napoleon wrasse and even hammerhead shark.

Time off from, or in between, boat dives guests can be found snorkelling or diving the *house reef*. Always close by, you can step off the jetty or swim to the reef edge. It drops sharply to thirty metres and is recovering well.

Unsurprisingly the rhythms of the resort reflect the schedule of the divers: morning dive, lunch, afternoon dive, shower, relax on the beach, beer, dinner, bed. For this reason, there is not a big take-up of the organised excursions.

Relative price:

10

7

Density of
rooms to
island size:

Those who aren't diving have the **beach** to themselves during the day, for tanning and reading, or sleeping in the shade. And it's an excellent beach for it. From the shade outside the rooms to the shallow lagoon the sand is deep, white and fine. Despite the usual seasonal erosion, it also travels, unimpeded, all around the island.

Time off from boat dives means diving or snorkelling the house reef.

There are forty six individual bungalows divided between standard, superior and deluxe. All the **rooms** were renovated in 1996 under the new ownership. They are all clean, white, simple and adequately decorated. The standard rooms do not have air conditioning or hot water (and even the water in the deluxe room was not really hot), but that is the only grumble. Not all rooms are on the beach, some are tucked behind. The deluxe rooms have minibars.

The interior of the island is not attractive, with the service area, a concrete

five-a-side football pitch and few good trees. So no need to linger on the way to the restaurant or bar. The public buildings are kept to a minimum, with the bar doubling as the coffee shop and disco floor. The beer is fairly priced at $2.75, but a bottle of water is overpriced.

Most of the guests are on **full board**, with some half board. Breakfast and dinner are buffet, lunch is set and surprisingly good; mostly fish and chicken, but well prepared.

Understandably there are a large number of repeaters among the guests; most of whom are German speakers, with the remainder mainly British and Japanese.

Resort	tel: 450587 fax: 450558
	email:bir0587@dhivehinet.net.mv

can of beer: $2.75	half day-
lime juice: $3.30	island hopping: $12
mineral water: $5.50	sunset fishing: $12

Dive centre	Mal-dive Centre
	single dive, all equipment: $55
	five dives, all equipment: $275
	certified open water course: $400+

BIYADOO

Flying.....n/a
Speed boat.....60 mins
Dhoni.....n/a

South Malé Atoll

BIYADOO, LIKE ITS SISTER ISLAND VILLIVARU, is essentially a dive island. What distinguishes this resort is the quality of the dive base, the mature beauty of the island and its house reef and the professional skills of the Indian management.

The good soil of Biyadoo has given rise to as tall a group of coconut palms as you will see anywhere in the country. On top of a variety of other naturally growing palms and trees, the management has added papaya, mango, lime, guava, banana and more. Such soil quality is rare indeed in the Maldives.

Disappointingly, guests cannot wander all over the island. There is a well-defined, concrete bordered path running around the island just behind the rooms and guests are not allowed inside this. On the other hand, outside the path is everything the usual holidaymaker is interested in. And almost all of it concentrated in a hundred metre area near the main jetty.

To the right of the jetty as you come from the water is the dive centre, the watersports centre, the main beach and the café, restaurant and shop. To the left of the jetty is the reception and lounge and one of the two blocks of rooms. Only the second block of rooms (the sunrise block) is away from this area (connected by a path through the middle of the island).

The **dive centre** is larger than but otherwise identical to Villivaru's. They are among the most modern and best looking in the country. Both are PADI five star centres and both are very well run by friendly, multilingual staff. There

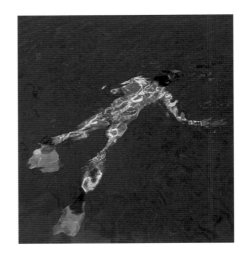

Relative price*

9

5

Density of rooms to island size:

is a good degree of freedom for the more experienced divers, even to the point of dives over one hour for those with bottom time and air remaining.

Diving in the region is some of the best of all the resort atolls

Biyadoo's dive base is so popular that boats leave four times a day, and they're all full. That may be off-putting, but then the diving in the region is some of the best of all the resort atolls. A short boat ride away are the dense schools of fish around Kandooma Thila, the soft corals of the huge Kandooma Caves, and the delights of the large Protected Marine Area, Guraidhoo Kandu.

Diving the **house reef** is also understandably popular. The coral is so thick around the island, and also so near, that six channels have been cut through to enable easy access to any part of the reef. Never too far from shore, its resident schools of several different fish, topographical variety and good coral re-growth means that it ranks as one of the best resort house reefs.

The **accommodation** is in two-storey blocks. There are six blocks, each with eight rooms above and eight rooms below (ninety six in all). The corner rooms are slightly larger and will take three or four beds for a family. Each block has good shade cover and a reasonable beach.

The **beach** comes and goes around the

island, but there is plenty for everyone and good opportunities to find your own 'hideaway' beach between the palms and bushes. And, for a diving island, there is a long list of different excursions.

The resort is **full board** only. Breakfast and lunch are buffets, dinners are set, but with a choice of chicken, fish or meat. Every few days, for a $20 supplement, there is an evening buffet special. The Indian chef cooks good, tasty food.

Resort	tel: 447171	fax: 447272
	email:resvn@biyadoo.com.mv	
can of beer: $2.00	full day	
lime juice: $1.50	island hopping: $45	
mineral water: $3.00	sunset fishing: $20	

Dive centre	Jurgen Schaegger's
	single dive, all equipment: $37
	ten dives, all equipment: $340
	certified open water course: $462

BODUHITHI

The island has good natural growth but only two significant beaches. This, however, is all that seems to be required. One beach is around the main jetty, in front of the bar/lounge. This is the 'noisy' beach where everybody congregates for canoeing and windsurfing, water aerobics, dancing on the beach (to music from the bar) and general lively interaction.

The 'quiet' beach is on the northern tip of the island and is a large, wide open stretch of white sand. It is also popular but there are no boats, boards or music. This is the spot for getting down to serious sun-tanning. Most of the rest of the island is walled in. The low, cement-topped, coral wall is not too unattractive and it is broken up by occasional steps down to the shallow water and soft sand.

The lagoon has good variety: sometimes near and sometimes far (mostly near), with deep areas and shallow. The snorkelling, however, is only OK as the reef edge is still on the way back from a crown of thorns starfish infestation a few years ago. There are good diving sites to be found in the neighbourhood, but diving is by no means a priority on this resort.

∿ BODUHITHI IS THE LARGEST OF CLUB VACANZA'S FIVE resorts in the country and the only one that is still very much in the 'club' style. All the guests are Italian, there are lots of organized activities and there are twenty Italian staff members whose job is to get everyone involved.

Relative price:

6

8

Density of
rooms to
island size:

The rooms are essentially the same as the other Club Vacanza rooms. They are very well specified, with two wash basins, hairdryer, bidet, large mirrors, telephones and minibar. The furniture is of dark wood and dark varnished cane and the fittings are of good quality. But the build quality was not perfect (gaps in the bathroom tiles, an ill-fitted plastic shower rail).

As always, the food is excellent. The meals are buffet and the selection is comprehensive. There is always a choice of pasta dishes, plus plenty of salads and fruits. The tables sit eight, so guests mix and meet in an easy way.

After lunch and dinner there are entertainments in the lounge, usually some participatory dance, quiz or request game. In the evening there is also a cabaret, fashion show or disco.

The general atmosphere is not at all snobby or exclusive, but friendly and easy-going. The resort is run smoothly in a relaxed manner. As long as you know what you are letting yourself in for when you book a holiday here, you will thoroughly enjoy it.

Resort   *tel*: 443981   *fax*: 442634
    email:hcmmale@clubvacanza.com.mv

    can of beer: $ incl.   half day-
        lime juice: $ incl.   island hopping: $incl.
    mineral water: $ incl.   sunset fishing: $incl.

Dive centre   Boduhithi
        single dive, all equipment: $incl.
            five dives, all equipment: $incl.
        certified open water course: $400

BOLIFUSHI

Flying......n/a
Speed boat......30 mins
Dhoni......70 mins

South Malé Atoll, north-west

〜〜 IF YOU ARE LOOKING FOR A SMALL, FRIENDLY, WELL- priced resort not far from Malé, Bolifushi is a strong option.

Although only fifteen kilometres from the airport, it is alone in the north west corner of South Malé Atoll, so one gets the sense of being out on the edge.

In 1999 the forty three rooms (Boli rooms and Beach Bungalows) were renovated and eight water bungalows added to the total. Every room is clean, bright and larger than expected (two extra beds can be put in). There is a telephone in each room, good fittings and hot, fresh water. The eleven beach rooms , made of coral, wood and thatch, are pleasant, quiet and comfortable. Some may feel that there are now too many rooms on such a small island.

But perhaps not the Italians who make up the largest number of guests. Germans, Swiss and Japanese are the others. You may feel confident in the hands of the experienced manager, Georgio Lagorio.

Because of the size of the island and the nature of the people who come here, everybody gets known by sight quickly and the place usually gels into a friendly club. The well-designed **bar and coffee shop** over the water is the evening meeting point where something is going on every night. The regular events are Bodu Beru, magic

show, fire limbo, calypso band, crab race and table tennis tournament. But though friendly, it is essentially a calm island so the partying doesn't go on too late.

The island, pointing in a north/south

direction, has a sunrise **beach** and a sunset beach. Neither are long, but they are both fairly wide. Then again, there are more people sharing them. There is good variety in the lagoon: shallow/deep, sandy/'corally'.

The **reef edge** itself is excellent for both snorkelling and diving. There is even a small wreck gathering coral and schools of fish. Beginners should be careful of the strong currents at this western edge. The diving in the wider region is mostly concentrated in the north and east of the atoll. The boats here are never full.

The **watersport** centre is particularly well stocked with new equipment. And Bolifushi is lucky enough to have a spotless sand bank just a pleasant

catamaran or windsurf ride away.

The food is fine but nothing special. Breakfast is a basic spread, lunch is set (plentiful but ordinary) and the evening meal is a buffet. The **restaurant** itself is a light, open-sided building, both simple and elegant.

This is a simple, straightforward island, without pretensions but with plenty of good vibes.

Resort	tel: 443517	fax: 445924
	email:admin@bolifushi.com	

can of beer: $2.50	half day-
lime juice: $3.50	island hopping: $25
mineral water: $3.00	sunset fishing: $15

Dive centre Atoll Diving Tours
single dive, all equipment: $50
five dives, all equipment: $250
certified open water course: $415

CLUB MED

Flying......n/a
Speed boat......15 mins
Dhoni......35 mins

North Malé Atoll

∿ CLUB MED IS DEAD, LONG LIVE THE CLUB MEDS!

The original Club Med island has been subsumed into the greater Hulumale' project (airport island landfill). In its place two Club Meds are opening. One is being built from scratch on Raa atoll and should be open for 2002. The other opened in November 2000 on what used to be its neighbour resort of Kanifinolhu.

As well as location, the two islands shared the same size, shape and philosophy, so the choice was natural and the switch was smooth. The philosophy is the same as Club Meds around the world: an active holiday, excellent cuisine and a club atmosphere in a beautiful setting. Kanifinolhu had all these ingredients except really first rate food. A brand new kitchen and new chefs have brought fine eating to the island in the shape of French and Japanese cuisine (predominantly). The breads, cheeses and desserts are maybe the best anywhere in the country.

A multi-lingual animation team do an excellent job of explaining, entertaining and bringing people into the 'Club'. This is not done in the old pushy way, but by genial encouragement to take part in the daytime fun and games, the multiple watersports and the nightly participation shows.

In the high season the guests are a complete mix of Europeans and Japanese. During the summer holiday months of July and August French are the most significant group, while from September to December it's the Japanese.

As an all-inclusive resort, the watersports equipment and tutoring is free. This is one of only a few resorts with good surfing. Waterskiing and deep-sea fishing are also available but must be paid for.

The lagoon facing into the atoll is large and reasonably deep and so good for watersports. On the other hand the reef edge is not reachable from the either side of the island and so snorkeling is not convenient. Group trips are organised to local reefs.

The beach facing into the atoll is partly man-made (almost everyone does some dredging now) which means it is not of the very finest sand and it is somewhat compacted – being flat too only helps the beach volleyball. It is very broad and shady under lines of teenage coconut palms. The beach on the other side faces out to the open ocean and is consequently smaller and

Relative price:

6

7

Density of
rooms to
island size:

*Club Med's new home
in Male' Atoll, the former
Kanifinolhu*

Resort	tel: 444552	fax: 441997
	email:	

can of beer: 'beads'	half day-
lime juice: 'beads'	island hopping: 1 incl.
mineral water: 'beads'	sunset fishing: 1 incl.

Dive centre Club Med
single dive, all equipment: 1 incl.
five dives, all equipment: $
certified open water course: $

also slightly rough, but really nothing to complain about.

The rooms won't be receiving many complaints either. They are all solid, well-appointed and very well decorated. Forty six water bungalows rooms (twenty three pairs) have been especially built for Club Med. Made entirely of wood and, again, beautifully decorated, they are a treat for the eyes. Built in a complete semi-circle from East, through South, to West some face the morning sun, some the setting sun and others the sun all day. But these southern facing ones also face the inhabited island of Huraa, just a couple of hundred metres away.

Maldives and Club Med are an excellent match so I am sure this new location will prove popular and this Club Med will have a long life.

CLUB RANNALHI

Flying.....n/a
Speed boat.....45 mins
Dhoni.....150 mins

South Malé Atoll

〜〜 **THIS COMPLETELY REBUILT RESORT** opened in 1996. The word 'club' is important because this is one of the most clubby, let's-all-do-it-together resorts in the country. It also reflects the importance of I Viaggi del Ventaglio, who have three quarters of the rooms and whose other resorts worldwide are called Club Venta. Although Italians make up some eighty per cent, French make up around thirteen per cent and Germans and British the rest.

There seem to be **activities** and **music** most of the day and into the night. It could be aqua gym, bocha, volleyball, Latin dancing, quizzes or a number of other fun, participatory events. The active watersports centre on the main beach, offers canoeing, windsurfing, water-skiing and banana boat rides.

The **diving** school is large and enthusiastic. It is one of the very few centres that organise three dives a day: either two in the morning and one in the afternoon, or one in the morning, one in the afternoon and a night dive. With a high instructor to guest ratio, they have the opportunity to take first timers on discovery dives, as well as run PADI courses and even skin diving courses.

The **beaches** are good almost all the way around, both wide and fine-grained. The lagoon is very good too, sandy-bottomed close to shore but with decent coral

Relative price:

8

8

Density of
rooms to
island size:

growth at the reef edge, which is never too far to swim to.

The only problem, for many people, will be the number of **rooms**. The reception, restaurant and coffee shop are gathered together in a spacious area, with lovely sand in-between. But the one hundred land rooms are in tightly packed, two-storey blocks. Then there are sixteen water bungalows as well. If you are

gregarious you might think this works out just fine, otherwise you probably won't.

Activities and music most of the day and into the night

The blocks are made of concrete, but they are attractively painted. Inside, the rooms are on the small side and the furniture is only OK, but the facilities are good: hot and cold water, a/c, minibar, hairdryer and two showers. Each opens onto a beach or a balcony.

The **restaurant** serves three buffets a day, including regular theme evenings. Overall, the food is not as good as some other Italian resorts who spend more importing direct from Europe, but there are, it seems, few complaints.

As indeed there are few complaints about the holidays here in general. A new company in the Maldives is running this new resort and the results are all that could be expected and better.

Nonetheless, you should be fun-loving, and perhaps Italian too, to really enjoy it here.

Resort	tel: 442034	fax: 442035
	email:reserve@rannalhi.com.mv	
can of beer: $3.30	half day-	
lime juice: $4.40	island hopping: $25	
mineral water: $3.85	sunset fishing: $12	
Dive centre	Venta	
	single dive, all equipment: $53	
	five dives, all equipment: $250	
	certified open water course: $330+	

Coco Palm

Flying.....30 mins
Speed boat.....n/a
Dhoni.....n/a

Baa Atoll

〜 COCO PALM IS ONE OF THE NEW RESORTS THAT IS trying to challenge the best of the established resorts. Built quickly, it will take a few years yet to fulfill its potential.

Although not central to most people's holiday, the lack of good vegetation lets the place down. Efforts are obviously being made and one corner of the island has a remarkable jungle, but there is also plenty of untidy and patchy low growth of bushes and plants.

Mature gardening will help to hide one room from another; important on this island because there is a high density of rooms to land area. This has resulted in some rooms being tucked behind one or more other rooms.

That said, the rooms themselves are very pleasant. At present there are essentially three categories: beach villa (58), deluxe villa (26) and lagoon villa (12). Sometime before the end of 2001 some rooms will be upgraded to an extra deluxe villa standard. The beach and deluxe villas vary only in luxury details: four posts on the bed, a sunken bath and a hammock and splash pool outside. The deluxe villas are, however, positioned close to the snorkeling area.

The lagoon villas are the same size as the other two categories but are more luxurious still in terms of the furniture and materials used. Beautifully put together they are intimate and private. Six of them look North and six look

South, while another two at the end of the walkway look West to the sunset. These are the lagoon palace suites, the pinnacle of accommodation on the island. All the rooms have steps down to the lagoon which, on this side, doesn't have corals but is perfect for swimming: deep and sandy.

The snorkeling is on the other side of the island where the reef edge comes close enough to swim to easily. Even without going to the drop off there are enough coral clumps in the lagoon on this side to attract plenty of fish and keep the novice happy.

Diving is not a big draw here, but as the only resort in the south and west of the

Relative price:

4

8

Density of
rooms to
island size:

atoll the sites are certainly fresh. Local thilas are the mainstay and the highlights as coral regrowth becomes more and more obvious.

The beach runs right around the island (except for one corner in the low season) and the sand is wonderful, as fine and soft as anywhere in the country. When not soaking up the sun you might head to the recreation centre for its snooker, table tennis, gym and jacuzzi. Nearby are the badminton, volleyball and tennis courts. And then there is the spa run by the world-famous Mandara Spa company.

Or, of course, you could go to the bar. The lagoon bar is going to enlarge and change to become far more attractive and to include an over-the-water grill. This will be the place for your sundowner. The main bar is huge and without a view to beach or water.

Aware that the place could do with a bit more intimacy, the large restaurant will be screened into more cozy areas. There can be no complaints about the food, however. Arrayed on three small dhonis, the three courses are each as good as each other. For a romantic change, a fine seafood grill is open every evening.

And talking of romance, there are two excursions that are particularly enticing. One is a champagne breakfast, or sunset cocktail, on your own isolated sandbank. The other is a dinner barbecue on an uninhabited island. After which the two of you are left alone for the night, with just a walkie-talkie for emergencies.

Resort	*tel*: 230011	*fax:* 230022
	email: cocopalm@dhivehinet.net.mv	

can of beer: $3.30	half day-
lime juice: $4.40	island hopping: $25
mineral water: $3.85	sunset fishing: $12

Dive centre Ocean Pro
single dive, all equipment: $63
five dives, all equipment: $315
certified open water course: $480+

DHIGUFINOLHU

Flying.....n/a
Speed boat.....35 mins
Dhoni.....90 mins

South Malé Atoll

〰〰 **A** FINE NEW MANAGE-
MENT TEAM IS TURNING
Dhigufinolhu into a very good resort; a
clean, well-organised, value-for-money
place that has 'pros' and 'cons' but is
constantly improving.

Its an odd thing but the 'pros' and 'cons'
are often related. For example, the
snorkeling is bad but the diving is
excellent. The reef edge is inaccessible
and there's not much in the lagoon, but
only a few minutes on the dive dhoni
brings you to a wreck, a manta point, a
shark point and a spectacular cave. A
bonus is the dive base leader, Jorge
Aebe, who is not only friendly and vastly
experienced, but one of the country's
best underwater photographers. His
weekly slide show is a knockout. And as
to the snorkeling, four trips a week go to
nearby sites; if there is more demand,
then more trips are possible.

Snorkeling is also possible on the large
platform, nicknamed Alcatraz, that is set
at one edge of the reef. This is only
accessible by boat, which you must hail
by waving a flag from the bar at the
centre of the long walkways. The walkways connect Dhigufinolhu with the
other three islands in the same lagoon.

The lagoon, being large and very shallow,
is not great, but the beaches are superb.
Soft, wide and ubiquitous they are real
plus point. Dhigufinolhu actually means
long sandbar. It also indicates a lack of
palm trees and shade, but now, with time
and good gardening, there is a decent
growth of palms, plenty of shade and
lovely flowers. And, with the manager a
keen gardener, it's set to improve further.

One unadulterated 'pro' is the food. A
priority of the manager (himself a chef),
the buffets are extensive, varied and

Relative price

7

9

Density of
rooms to
island size:

imaginative. "Que mangare!" was heard from one full and satisfied Italian. Furthermore, nowhere is the quality of produce more carefully monitored all the way down the line and the kitchens are so hygienic they have an 'open day' once a week for guests to look around themselves.

The Dolphin Grill is a small, romantic restaurant set apart on the sunset beach. Traditional and imaginative dishes based around seafood (ravioli of prawns with crustacean sauce) are served in a distinctly superior setting. Better still, the prices take into account, in a generous manner, money already paid for

full or half-board. So a pepper steak may cost you $3, a soup may be $1 and a fine, three course meal might total $10.

The new room service is part of a steady upgrading of the rooms. The superior rooms (27) are good but the standard rooms (73) are disappointing. In time the old-fashioned, 'heavy' textiles will be modernised and the minimal, cheap furniture and lighting will be changed.

This resort used to be mostly Swiss and German, then mostly Italian, and now it is a little over half Swiss and German, a little over one third Italian and about a fifth British and French. The mix works

fine. There are a lot of activities organised for the day and the evening, which suits the Italians well. But the animation is 'soft' (the really 'clubby' Italians go to Bodu Huraa next door), and the general atmosphere is one of calm and relaxation.

Resort	tel: 443599 fax: 44886
	email: dhigufinolhu@palmtree.com.mv

can of beer: $3.85	half day-
lime juice: $3.85	island hopping: $15
mineral water: $3.30	sunset fishing: $15

Dive centre	Scubasub
	single dive, all equipment: $60
	five dives, all equipment: $300
	certified open water course: $450+

EMBUDU VILLAGE

Flying.....n/a mins
Speed boat.....n/a mins
Dhoni.....45 mins

South Malé Atoll

∿ EMBUDU VILLAGE ENJOYS A HIGH RETURN RATE OF

satisfied customers. The reason for that is the successful way the resort takes the middle ground. That is, the buildings are smart, almost formal, but there is sand on the floors, encouraging you to be shoeless and informal; the service is attentive and efficient, but also friendly; there are carefully tended gardens and paths, but the place still remains relaxed and easy going.

As the manager says, tourists have been demanding more quality over the years but they still want the informality of a sun-drenched island. A number of resorts do this well, Embudu Village is certainly one of them.

There used to be more standard *rooms* than superior rooms, but now there are seventy two superiors and thirty six standards. The main differences are air conditioning, a little more space and the odd piece of furniture. Both types of rooms are not particularly attractive from the outside (corrugated iron roof, small terrace and two plastic chairs), but inside they are well lit, high-ceilinged and white, with solid, well varnished wood. There is fresh water in the tap and shower, but hot water in the shower only (and a bit weak).

The sixteen water bungalows are correctly described as deluxe: large, simply and well furnished, with a telephone, minibar, satellite tv, and a glass panel in the wood-lined floor to see the fish and coral below. No other island has water bungalows so close to such a coral

garden. In fact, the coral is so close (to the bungalows and to the surface) that steps could not be built down from the balconies. (You just can't have everything!)

The **snorkelling** is terrific all around the island. The house reef has an abundance of corals and schools of fish, and is close to shore for most of the way around.

The resort is a successful blend of an up-market look and an informal atmosphere

The **beach**, on the other hand, gets rather thin around some of the island, but at the three 'points' of this triangular island the sand bulges out into the lagoon. One of these three fine beaches faces due west and so is perfect for watching the sun go down.

Diving is popular and enjoyable here. Popular because of the variety of great dives nearby, and enjoyable because the dive base leaders and staff are particularly friendly and accommodating, as well as efficient. The Protected Marine Area of Embudu Channel is a couple of minutes

Relative price:

9

10

Density of
rooms to
island size:

away and encompasses the thrilling drift dive of Embudu Express, the coral gardens of Embudu Thila and a shark point (grey reef sharks).

The resort has a °majority of German guests, with a significant proportion of French as well as Austrians, Dutch, Swiss and Japanese. Everybody is on full board, with a buffet breakfast and dinner and set lunch. The **restaurant**, with its metal roof and insufficient fans, is rather hot, but the service and the food are good. Two nights a week there are specials outside - either steak, prawns or lobster - which cost extra but are attractively laid out.

Finally, excursions are well advertised and well organised. Being close to Malé and the airport is convenient for the shopping trips and the photo-flights.

Embudu has a high density of rooms, but it is a pretty island and excellently managed.

Resort	tel: 444776 fax: 442673
	email: embvil@dhivehinet.net.mv
can of beer: $3.00	full day-
lime juice: $2.60	island hopping: $24
mineral water: $3.50	sunset fishing: $13

Dive centre	Diverland Embudu
	single dive, all equipment: $40
	six dives, all equipment: $228
	certified open water course: $455

EQUATOR VILLAGE

Flying.....90 mins
Speed boat.....n/a
Dhoni.....n/a

Addu Atoll

〜〜 **EQUATOR VILLAGE HAS ONE BIG DIFFERENCE FROM ALL THE** other resorts in the Maldives. This resort is not an island on its own, but a small part of a large island, which is itself connected to six other islands, inhabited and uninhabited.

This means it is the only resort where you can go off and freely mix with *'real life'*. Not for an hour or two on the day you are expected, but at any time. The real pleasure of this resort is cycling off to explore the other islands, to discover for yourself lovely beaches in quiet coconut groves and to casually meet the locals. The level of spoken English here is good, so there is an opportunity not just to look but to interact.

Germans make up the big majority of guests here, with some Russian parties as well as a few Italians and Swiss. Almost everybody is on all-inclusive. It should be said that the food is fairly basic and the drinks are not premium brands. But the usual atmosphere is excellent. Perhaps the unique situation of

the resort brings people together more than other places. The only actual organised evening entertainment is a weekly disco. But there is also table tennis, a full-size snooker table and a good tennis court.

It should also be said that the beach is nothing to write home about. It's there but narrow and broken up by coral groynes. You can cycle off to find a special spot on another island or you can join everyone else by the large, central, swimming pool.

Explore the other islands, to discover for yourself lovely beaches in quiet coconut groves.

The seventy eight **rooms** are in smart rows behind gardens of clipped grass and tropical flowers. Inside, they are cool and comfortable with a level of furnishing above what would be expected at this price level. Included is a minibar (filled

Relative price:

10

on request) and three mirrors, but no telephone (use the public phone booth). The grounds of the hotel, like the whole island of Gan, are wonderfully **green**, with a variety of indigenous and introduced trees and flowers (and bird life) not found on other islands.

Apart from providing bicycles, the resort runs a minibus for **excursions** along the connecting causeway up to the last island in the chain, Hithadu, the capital of the atoll. Here you can wander around, shop and eat lunch in a local restaurant. Dhoni trips are organised to visit the inhabited and uninhabited islands on the other side of the atoll, where there is

good snorkeling to be had before a barbecue on the beach.

The ability to see Maldivian life, in as large or as small a dose as you wish, is one of two good reason to come here. The other reason is to go diving.

By some fluke of channels and currents, the coral bleaching that affected the rest of the country simply did not happen here. So for outstanding coral gardens and walls this is the place. And for year-round mantas this is also the place. Indeed all the big fish are regulars hereabouts, including grey reef sharks, even tiger sharks, barracudas, tunas and napoleon wrasse.

The dives are mostly forty to fifty minutes away, so there are no more than two dives a day plus a weekly night dive, as well as any number of housereef dives. Inside the atoll the visibility is poor (so housereef snorkeling is not great) but one highlight is the one hundred and forty metre wreck 'British Royalty', the biggest in the country.

Resort	tel: 588721	fax: 588020
	email:	
can of beer: $incl.		full day-
lime juice: $incl.		island hopping: $1 incl.
mineral water: $incl.		sunset fishing: $1 incl.

Dive centre	Diverland
	single dive, all equipment: $41
	five dives, all equipment: $205
	certified open water course: $425

ERIYADU

Flying.....n/a
Speed boat.....50 mins
Dhoni.....n/a

North Malé Atoll

ᴔᴔTHE ONLY BUILDING LEFT STANDING AFTER ERIYADU'S refit is the thatched bar above the beach. Everything else is new. Happy former guests of Eriyadu, however, should not be upset. The island retains its simple style and quiet, easy-going atmosphere, it's just that the built surroundings are now of a much higher standard, and you have to pay a little more.

In common with many resorts, there are a number of rooms available over and above the quoted fifty seven, for overbooking problems. And Eriyadu already has a fairly high density of rooms to overall area, so this might be an issue

for some people, though it must be said that the situation is not obvious. A reason for this is that the pairs of rooms have a verandah wall between them and are staggered. Plus, though the island doesn't have a large number of coconut palms, there is a good growth of trees and bushes separating rooms and giving good shade between them and the beach.

Inside, the rooms are cool, dim and comfortable. The parquet flooring is dark hardwood from Malaysia, the cupbboards and tables too are dark brown with brass fittings. In addition to a safe and well-stocked minibar there is a four station radio on tap and a tv with satelite channels including DW, BBC, CNN and

ESPN. The bathroom is pretty basic: bath with plastic shower attachment, hairdryer, basin and a very small open area with another shower.

The restaurant is cleverly divided into two parts with different chairs and table cloths so the size (though relatively small anyway) is not apparent. In between is the buffet area for all meals. This is certainly an area of major improvement from past times. Now there is not only a greater choice but the food is notably well cooked (roast potatoes that are crisp, beef that is tender etc.).

About half of the guests are on half board and lunch is taken in the new

Relative price:

9

10

Density of
rooms to
island size:

Eriyadu enjoys almost perfect geography. That is, it is near the edge of the atoll so the dive sites are all close by, but it is protected from the strong outside currents, so the beaches are broad, fine and all-surrounding. There are no outer walls and just a few, solid beach-bound groynes.

coffee shop attached to the main bar. The food here is only ok but it does stay open until 11pm and, amazingly, it seems someone will get up at any time of night to cook a meal.

The all new, same old Eriyadu

The bar stays open till eleven every night and longer if anyone is still drinking. Entertainment is more geared towards the relax and watch type more than discos. This is often the case in islands with a large number of divers. More effort is put into entertainments in the low season, sensibly enough. A few steps away in the

reception building is an open room for darts and table tennis. In the same building is a pool room and excercise room.

Diving remains central to the resort. The new centre is on its own jetty a few metres from the boats. As Eriyadu is the last resort on the western side of the atoll the dive sites are relatively little visited and exceptionally good. Even the house reef is excellent for diving (and for snorkelling too despite the dead corals). Apart from the two jetties, there are three exits cut across the reef and a bench on the beach where the dive centre boys drop off and pick up your equipment.

Germans, Swiss and Austrians make up around three quarters of the guests, with Japanese, British and Italians making up the rest. In its former guise this resort had an unusually high rate of returns (read, satisfied customers) and I feel sure it will succeed again in its remodeled form.

Resort   tel: 444487   fax: 445926
email: eriyadu@aaa.com.mv

can of beer: $ half day-
lime juice: $ island hopping: $
mineral water: $ sunset fishing: $

Dive centre   Eriyadu
single dive, all equipment: $
five dives, all equipment: $
certified open water course: $

FESDU

Flying......25 mins
Speed boat......120 mins
Dhoni......n/a

Ari Atoll, north-central

one full-day excursion (resort, inhabited island and uninhabited island), one shopping trip, one snorkelling trip, a day fishing and a night fishing. On top of this normal selection there are a couple of unusual choices. Apparently you can choose to go on a real Maldivian fishing boat all day and try tuna fishing with a local crew. There is also a small, uninhabited island close by which you can book to be alone together for a day.

The evening **entertainments** are lively and go on longer than most, as guests enjoy the 'free' booze. The diving fraternity, however, sometimes feel short

The planted flowers bloom all around under the towering coconut palms

changed as they cannot drink too much and go diving the next morning.

Those that do get up to **dive** don't have to go far for their sport. The house reef itself has a great wall dive with octopus and rays, stone fish and lion fish, good coral cover and much more. Just a few minutes away is a coral outcrop with turtles and lobsters, and there is a great wreck dive a few minutes beyond that. Further on again is a site with some of the best cave diving in the atoll.

Those staying on the resort can lounge around on fine **beaches** that go right around the island. Naturally the beaches tend to shift around the island with the two monsoons, but here (again) a big effort is made to keep the beaches in place all year round. That means groynes (which are plentiful but not obstructive), sand dredging (from lagoon and beach), and/or walls (none here any longer).

Behind the fine beaches is a sandy path

IN MANY WAYS FESDU REFLECTS THE DEVELOPMENT of tourism in the Maldives. From the original camping style (when it opened in 1978) the resort has gone through many changes (the latest renovation was in 1996). Now it is a much more controlled environment, with most of the modern conveniences, yet it is still undeniably beautiful.

One of the modern changes is the switch to **all-inclusive** holidays only. On this resort that means: all food (including snacks from the bar and coffee shop), a wide selection of drinks, one excursion and watersports (snorkel/mask and windsurfers but no catamaran or canoe).

On a weekly basis there is one half-day excursion (resort and inhabited island),

Relative price:

7

9

Density of
rooms to
island size:

travelling around the island in front of the bungalows. This is a lovely walk in itself as planted *flowers* bloom all around under towering coconut palms. Though you probably wouldn't notice it, you are restricted to this perimeter, unable to go 'inside' the island.

There are sixty *rooms*. Fifty four are individual, thatched, wooden bungalows. There is also one block of two rooms and one block of four. Though the blocks are less attractive outside, the interiors are identical. Smart and clean, they have air conditioning but no telephone or minibar.

The other buildings on the island are just as attractive to look at. Thatch on top, wood on the sides and sand on the floor. The interior decor is not up to the same standard, but nobody seems to mind that. There are seven buffets during the week (three lunch and four dinners), the rest is set. I cannot say the food is particularly good, but if you are not a gourmet it will suffice.

Germans account for two thirds of the guests and British the other one third. On this pretty island everyone felt they had made the right choice.

Resort	*tel*: 450541	*fax*: 450547
	email: sales@unisurf.com	
can of beer: $4.40		half day-
lime juice: $4.40		island hopping: $21
mineral water: $4.40		sunset fishing: $16
Dive centre		Fesdu
	single dive, all equipment: $40	
	five dives, all equipment: $335	
	certified open water course: $340	

FIHALHOHI

Flying......n/a
Speed boat......75mins
Dhoni......n/a

South Malé Atoll

Now there is a mix of tour operators and different nationalities, though it remains family oriented. The island is ideal for children. Most important of all is the fact that there are lots of other children. Plus wide open beaches, a shallow lagoon and crucially, plenty of shade. The island is also large and 'open' (you are not restricted from going anywhere), so there is plenty to explore. And then there are the watersports, the play areas and the games corridor (between the restaurant and reception). Finally, a sympathetic and helpful management.

One point to consider is that there are now one hundred and twenty eight rooms on the island (standard, superior, deluxe), which is pushing the comfort zone. The standard rooms are just that: satisfactory interiors, fresh water but not hot, four to a thatched block. The superior rooms are larger than average, neat and simply decorated. These also have a telephone and a minibar.

Not all the rooms have beaches outside, but there is always a broad sandy area, in the shade of massive coconut palms, between the rooms and the water. This is perfect for lounging in a hammock and reading or keeping an eye on the children playing. Such a mature island with this variety and size of growth is rare in the Maldives. A telling sign is the large number of birds in the trees and at the water's edge.

The big **beaches** are on the west and north sides. Here the sand is like icing sugar and walking in the lagoon is like playing with the icing. Well placed on the west beach is the **watersports** centre adjoining the coffee shop and bar. This is the second 'centre' of the island. The large coffee shop has a very good selection of food and drinks on offer. The watersports are comprehensive and child friendly with special children's lessons. Apart from the windsurfers, catamarans

FIHALHOHI IS ONE OF THE BEST KEPT SECRETS IN THE Maldives. Although hardly ever talked about it is, in my opinion, the best budget family resort in the country. Perhaps the best budget resort full stop. A mix of natural beauty and holiday action.

There are a couple of reasons for the obscurity. One is that Fihalhohi is almost alone in the whole west and south-west of the atoll ('Club Rannalhi' is its only neighbour). The other reason is that a single German tour operator was, until 1998, the sole agent.

Relative price:

10

6

Density of
rooms to
island size:

*One of the best kept
secrets in the Maldives*

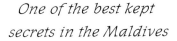

beginners, with some easy, shallow dives
which are beautiful but not intimidating.
The house reef itself is one of these and
is easily accessible from the shore.

The ***food*** is good to very good. The
breakfast buffet includes waffles and
home-made Danish pastries. Lunches are
also buffet. Four or five times a week the
dinner is a buffet outside. And what
variety! It could be Italian, barbecue,
Chinese, Mongolian, Sri Lankan or
Maldivian. And once a week, for an
additional charge, a seafood buffet is put
on at the coffee shop by the beach.

For families on a budget (whether
German, English, French or Italian) this
is the resort to book, if you can get it.

and canoes, there is water-skiing,
parasailing and banana boating.

Diving is not as popular as it used to be
before the emphasis on family holidays
began. However, not only are there some
excellent advanced dives around, but this
is also a particularly good area for

Resort	tel: 442903	fax: 443803
	email: fiha@dhivehinet.net.mv	

can of beer: $3.85	half day-
lime juice: $3.30	island hopping: $25
mineral water: $3.85	sunset fishing: $10

Dive centre	Ocean Venture
	single dive, all equipment: $57
	six dives, all equipment: $324
	certified open water course: $460

Filitheyo

Flying.....35 mins
Speed boat.....n/a
Dhoni.....n/a

Faafu Atoll

〜 FILITHEYO IS THE ONLY RESORT ON THIS ATOLL, JUST recently opened to tourism. As if capitalising on this fact it has attracted a high percentage of divers. But the wider truth is, it is a beautifully put together resort on a delightful island.

Five minutes away, on a diving dhoni, is the first of a string of channels going north. Along with the hidden tilas, these are ideal places to see the big fish. And being untouched to date, the general numbers of fish are truly impressive. One small disappointment is having to go an hour and a quarter to a manta point. And the search for a grey reef shark point continues. One novelty offered by the dive school is scooter diving, for groups of four.

The housereef is also excellent for diving and snorkeling, with a good wall on one side, a massive drop off on the other and plenty of fish. Six clear channels are cut through to the reef edge and boys from the dive centre will lug your gear to and from whichever one you choose.

The lagoon is narrow on one side (so the

reef edge is close) and broad on the other. The beaches follow the same pattern, narrow, but always decent, where the lagoon is small and wide where the lagoon is wide. The deluxe rooms are on the side with the better beach (and nearer the public buildings), but this is also where the lagoon is shallowest, and at low tide that is about a metre. Furthermore, it contains a lot of what used to be delightful live coral, but which is now sharp dead coral.

Apart from their location, the fifteen deluxe rooms difer from the ninety four superior rooms only because they have a bath tub, are fractionally bigger and are individual bungalows as opposed to semi-detached. There are also sixteen water bungalows. All the rooms are top class. The interior design gives a wonderfully

natural feel, though all the luxuries are here too. There is no plastic to be seen, even the chairs and loungers on the deck are solid wood. An unobtusive wooden cabinet hides a satelite television with DW, Rai and BBC among the channels. A discreet mini hifi is there, so bring along your cd's and cassettes. And even the minibar shows invention, with two cans of Murphy's Irish Stout, and carafes of red and white wine.

The whole resort is reminiscent of something south-east Asian and it works wonderfully. It comes together around the small, main bar. Wooden slatted

Relative price:

4

5

Density of
rooms to
island size:

walkways pass both sides of a lily pond and the sunken, cool and quiet library. The bar itself is delightfully 'rustic', but is passed by more often than not after dinner, as the next day's dive takes priority over evening entertainments.

German speakers are the large majority here, British make up around fifteen percent with a few Italians and Japanese and others making up the rest. Most people are on full board and its a good

choice, though not if you want to loose weight. A widely travelled Irish chef oversees a constantly changing, but always excellent, buffet selection. And only in Club Med have the desserts been this good (hot doughnuts, peanut icecream, fresh waffles...)

On one tip of the island is the coffee shop, sunset bar and swimming pool. Sipping a cappuchino you can look out passed the pool and the beach to the

lagoon, reef edge, open sea and sky - a classic harmony of blues. And that's one thing you'll never be on Filitheyo.

Resort	*tel*: 460025	*fax*: 460024
	email: fili@aaa.com.mv	

can of beer: $4.00	half day-
lime juice: $4.00	island hopping: $25
mineral water: $3.00	sunset fishing: $25

Dive centre	Werner Lau
	single dive, all equipment: $60
	five dives, all equipment: $295
	certified open water course:

FOUR SEASONS

Flying.....n/a
Speed boat.....25 mins
Dhoni.....n/a

North Malé Atoll

SITTING BY YOUR OWN SMALL POOL, SIPPING CHILLED white wine, breathing in the frangrance of an equatorial garden, time loses any relevance and concerns slip away. Four Seasons have brought five star magic to Kuda Huraa that fifteen long years ago was the closest Maldives came to a backpackers hangout. Today it looks as good as any resort in the very top bracket and its service is quite easily the best there is.

The staff, it seems, are well looked after and this translates to extraordinary attention to the needs, wishes and whims of each guest. There is a level of communication – information delivery, timely conversation, attentive listening – that other resorts just don't reach. The end result is guests truly at their ease.

The same attention to the details of service is there in the details of landscaping and interior décor.

This is not an island of native jungle but of crafted beds of local flowers and bushes, of fragrant night jasmine and frangipani, of many-hued hibiscus and rose. But not every room yet has its share of mature growth and most of the planted palm trees are teenagers still.

Fourteen beach bungalows have a wonderful enclosure of broad-leaved plants around a plunge pool, bleached wood deck and bougainvillea-shaded day bed. The single Kuda Huraa beach villa enjoys a larger and more luxuriantly-planted version of the same thing. The other beach bungalows (41 including six with outside showers) open directly to the resort, although facing away from any activity.

Inside, the rooms are furnished with an impeccable simplicity. The wardrobe is sunk back into the wall, the minibar, tv and vcd player are concealed in understated light wooden cupboards. The careful lighting, soft cotton fabrics and mutted colours soothe; the exotic, flowery outside shower delights.

For views, however, you must choose a water bungalow. These thirty four rooms have a floor-to-ceiling view across the lagoon from the bedroom, a picture window by the bath and, of course, a private verandah. The four Navaranna water villas are over twice as big, have two bathrooms and delight in an interior décor of exquisite minimalism.

Steps lead down from the verandahs to the lagoon. But the lagoon is not great: it is large, shallow, almost without corals. This means there is no snorkeling to speak of and, it must be said, even swimming is a little tricky when the current rushes in and out at the turning of the tides.

Then, to finish the bad news, the beaches are poor. Erosion reduces the width and myriad coral pieces underfoot make sandals essential, though the west beach, looking into the atoll, is better in this respect (and worse for sea grass).

Still, the large swimming pool, that seems to flow directly into the lagoon, is superb, the real focus of the island with its swim-up bar and two of the three restaurants nearby. Dining at the poolside is popular in the evening, an extension of the brasserie-style Café Huraa. The Baraabaru is the real specialty restaurant, serving classics and variations of South Asian cuisine. The third restaurant has a fine Mediterranean menu. The wine list is not that impressive but the food is faultless. And the service is second to none.

Relative price:

1

8

Density of rooms to island size:

Resort	*tel*: 444888	*fax*: 441188
	email: info@kudahuraa.com	

can of beer: $5.50   half day-
lime juice: $6.05   island hopping: $46
mineral water: $4.40   sunset fishing: $24

Dive centre   Four Seasons
single dive, all equipment: $71
six dives, all equipment: $403
certified open water course: $594

FULL MOON BEACH

Flying.....n/a
Speed boat.....20 mins
Dhoni.....45 mins

North Malé Atoll

JUST A FEW MINUTES BOAT RIDE FROM THE AIRPORT,

Full Moon Beach has been rebuilt to fulfil the dreams and expectations of a cosmopolitan business class. If you are looking for the barefoot, laid back, original Maldives style then this resort is not for you. What you get here is luxury: all the facilities of a modern resort, along with good looks and five star hotel service.

Facilities, good looks and service come together around the *swimming pool*. The largest and probably the best looking pool in the country it is at least as popular as the beach. Drinks are served at the poolside from the adjoining main bar, which itself is very comfortable and has a delightful sundeck over the shallows of the lagoon where baby sharks can be seen.

Across the ornamental bridge from the pool are the main public buildings. Facilities include a karaoke lounge, a piano bar and a fully equipped business centre with internet. The buildings are all solidly built in a sort of monumental style, with columns, wooden beams and bougainvilia. There is now also a new Serena Spa, with ayurvedic specialties.

The bougainvilia is just a small part of the resort's floral landscape. With a full-time horticulturalist and an army of gardeners all the public areas are beautifully decorated. Not particularly Maldivian but certainly attractive.

On this bell shaped island the wide end is reserved for the service area and the two sides have all the *rooms*. Down one side run the fifty two water bungalows, and down the other run the one hundred and

four beach rooms (in two-storey blocks of four). All the rooms are of a high standard with a/c and hot water, a bath, hair dryer, minibar and telephone.

The *beach* in front of the rooms is broad and long, but not of the very highest quality. The fact is that the beaches on the island have mostly been manufac-

Relative price:

6

9

Density of rooms to island size:

tured by dredging out sand from the lagoon and other areas. This results in a coarser grain of coral sand; entirely satisfactory of course, just not ideal.

The *lagoon* all around is pleasant for swimming, but although there are some good coral areas it is too large for easy snorkelling access. The gradually sloping lagoon is ideal for learning to dive and, for a non 'diving island', *diving* is fairly popular here, but that is understandable

with thirty regular and forty possible sites within a fifty five minute radius.

For further action there is the sports centre with tennis court, gym, sauna and jacuzzi (and piped music, as everywhere). These facilities are not heavily used, but they are there if you want them. What people mostly want is to enjoy the luxury of doing very little. The children have a new play area for themselves. One of the more difficult choices is deciding which

restaurant to go to. The main one is not as good as it might be, but there are four other, specialist, restaurants to try out.

Resort	tel: 442011	fax: 441979
	email: sales@unisurf.com	

can of beer: $4.40	full day-
lime juice: $4.40	island hopping: $44
mineral water: $4.40	sunset fishing: $22

Dive centre Full Moon
single dive, all equipment: $47
five dives, all equipment: $220
certified open water course: $450

Fun Island

Flying.....n/a
Speed boat.....45 mins
Dhoni.....n/a

South Malé Atoll

Beyond the friendly and efficient front office staff, in this spacious (if rather formal looking) building, are the shops, table tennis table, snooker room, karaoke room and gym. Beside these is the coffee shop/ à la carte restaurant and then the main restaurant.

With most of the activity taking place in this central area the rest of the island is quiet and

peaceful. Because it is such a thin island, the blocks of *rooms* are just about back to back, with half looking out eastward to the ocean and half looking westward into the atoll. The rooms are all the same: clean, white and simply decorated. They each have air conditioning, a minibar and good lighting. The bathrooms are bright and clean with very good fittings.

∿∿ FUN ISLAND HAS NOT BEEN VERY WELL ENDOWED BY

nature, but the effort put into it by man has turned it into a happy resort with great service and facilities, and plenty of activities. All at a very reasonable price.

As you come down the long jetty the island is laid out before you. To the left and right the beaches stretch away down the flank of this *long, thin island*, with the rooms just behind. In front of you is the group of smart, modern-looking 'public buildings'. The comfortable, open-sided main bar is just to the right, looking out over the lagoon.

The low line of identical rooms divided by white walls looks featureless from the outside, but that has a lot to do with the island itself. 'Bodufinolhu', the original name of the island means 'big island with few coconut palms'. The soil here is shallow and sandy and although much has been planted it all grows slowly and with difficulty.

The *beaches*, though, are generally very good. Anywhere on the island you can step out of your room and lie down on soft, fine-grained sand. The *lagoon* is

huge and shallow on all sides. This makes it pleasant for swimming and splashing about, but no good for *snorkeling*. The only place to do this from is the end of the jetty. Here people congregate, amicably passing the time of day sunning, chatting and snorkelling.

Not a high percentage of people dive here, but those that do really enjoy it. The *dive school* is run by a very experienced team in a most pleasant, patient and friendly manner. The dives are well conducted in small groups. And the channels just north of here around Guraidhoo and Kandooma offer some of the best diving in the country.

No pretensions, just a fun island

Fun Island also has an active and well-stocked **watersports** centre. You can hire or have lessons on the catamarans, windsurfers, canoes and water-skis, not forgetting the banana boat. Within the same lagoon are two pretty, uninhabited islands just far enough away to give your efforts a rewarding goal.

Relative price:

8

Density of rooms to island size:

8

All the usual fishing and island hopping excursions are organised during the day, and there is usually something going on in the main bar in the evening, from crab racing to live bands twice a week.

The main **restaurant** is big, but the food has not been compromised. Both the set meals and buffets, which alternate, are excellent. There is variety and quality and even some surprises. The good food surely contributes to the general atmosphere of well-being.

Contributing also to this positive atmosphere is the sense of **value for money**. Holidays here *can* be surprisingly

cheap as room occupancy is kept high as a priority. So the resort is usually full, but everyone is having a fun time.

Resort	tel: 444558 fax: 443958
	email: vilahtls@dhivehinet.net.mv
can of beer: $3.30	half day-
lime juice: $3.30	island hopping: $30
mineral water: $3.85	sunset fishing: $40
Dive centre	Delphis
	single dive, all equipment: $58
	six dives, all equipment: $348
	certified open water course: $585

GANGEHI

GANGEHI IS A BEAUTIFUL RESORT EXCLUSIVELY RUN BY Club Vacanza of Italy. There is just one drawback: major sand displacement in the last few years.

The former manager, Monica, set the calm, adult atmosphere that still pervades the place. She came to the Maldives when it all began, in 1972, so her experience is unmatched, with ten years here and ten years before that in Alimatha, she has now moved on to Kuda Rah. This resort continues to enjoy a high rate of guest returns and a very high rate of staff retention. This is so important for continuity and that wonderful 'welcome back' feel.

The rooms, restaurant and bar/lounge are first class. The bar/lounge rests on stilts over the water facing both south for the sun during the day, and west for the sunset. Its decor of dark brown and white cotton give it an air of cool comfort, accentuated by the large aquarium tank in the middle and various pieces of antique Indian furniture.

The **restaurant** looks out onto the vast west beach. The food is excellent. Breakfast and lunch are large buffets, dinners are served at the table. All the drinks are free in this truly **all-inclusive** resort. Service is personal and of a high standard (and includes twenty four hour room service).

The island's twenty five **rooms** are large and well put together. The theme again is dark wood, browns and whites. These are combined in Club Vacanza's textile design taken from the traditional Maldivian mats and used on bed covers and curtains. All the rooms are air conditioned and have a telephone and a minibar. The bathrooms are not large but they have quality

fixtures and fittings, including two wash basins, a bidet and a lovely, powerful old fashioned shower.

Eight of the twenty five rooms are water bungalows and these are a little larger than the others. Fourteen rooms are on the perimeter of the island and three are tucked away inside, particularly quiet and 'remote'.

'Remote' because the interior of the island feels like that. Winding through the virginal growth of mature trees and flowering shrubs is a well-built wooden walkway that feels like a nature trail through the shady greenery of the original Maldives.

The tragedy of the island is the bad joke that beach erosion has played on it. Over the last several years all the sand has shifted from the east side to the west side. This has left twelve bungalows with no **beach**, a low island wall and a wall in the lagoon to halt further erosion. At the same time the water bungalows (on the west side) no longer stand in water but on sand, and not only that but they and their walkways take up most of the only good beach. If only the water bungalows and beach bungalows were on opposite sides...

If you **dive** then this fairly expensive resort is still good value for money, as two dives a day are free; as well as all excursions. And not only are the dives as good as any others, but they are conducted in small groups with no competition for sites, as you are almost alone here in this quiet corner of the atoll.

Simply put, if it wasn't for the beach problem Gangehi would be one of the best resorts in the Maldives. As it is, it's is a great resort with one drawback.

Resort	tel: 450505	fax: 450506
	email: hcmmale@clubvacanza.com.mv	

can of beer: $incl.	half day-
lime juice: $incl.	island hopping: $incl.
mineral water: $incl.	sunset fishing: $incl.

Dive centre Club Vacanze
single dive, all equipment: $incl.
five dives, all equipment: $incl.
certified open water course: $400

GASFINOLHU

Flying.....n/a
Speed boat.....40 mins
Dhoni.....100 mins

North Malé Atoll

〰〰 **GASFINOLHU IS RUN BY VALTUR, THE ITALIAN HOLIDAY** company, which is similar to Club Vacanza or Club Med but is even more *'clubby'* and *active*. It is not a naturally pretty island, but the best has been made of it and the fun, 'all-together' atmosphere and the great food are the main ingredients of a holiday here.

The all-inclusive price covers quick transfer from the airport, full board and all sports except diving. There is no water-skiing available, but there are catamarans, canoes and windsurfers as well as beach petanque and darts. The *food* is wonderful. The three Italian chefs prepare a fine spread each day for the breakfast and lunch buffets and the evening set meal. The accent is very much on Italian cuisine of course. And every few days a particularly large and varied evening buffet is laid out.

The forty individual **bungalows** are light and quite large, though the shower room is small. The interiors are plain but pleasant enough and well built; there is

Relative pric
6

10

Density of
rooms to
island size:

no air condition-
ing, telephone or
minibar. Built of
coral stone and
thatch, in the
Maldivian manner,
they are
attractive from
the outside. And
indeed although
there isn't much
to the interior of
this very thin island, it is pleasing to the
eye, with its clean swept look and the
lily-lined path between bungalows.

Most things that happen on the island
happen on the **main beach** or in the bar/
lounge, which are situated either side of
the jetty. Everybody congregates here
throughout the day sunbathing, enjoying
the **watersports** or taking part in the
many **organised activities**. These include

water aerobics,
darts, petanque,
volleyball, table
tennis and cards.
There are lunch
time entertain-
ments by the
staff and evening
cabaret too.
Another regular
event is the
'fashion show'
displaying the clothes and wraps from
the resort shop.

If and when you want peace and quiet
the beaches on the other side of the
island are mostly unused and fine,
though they are rather small, in between
coral groynes. The swimming is good in
the shallow lagoon, but it is much too
big and empty for **snorkelling. Diving** is
not very popular here, though that means

The fun 'all-together'
atmosphere and the great
food are the main ingredients
of a holiday here

if you do want to go you will enjoy small
group diving and some first class sites
nearby, both for experienced divers and
for beginners.

Resort	*tel*: 442078	*fax*: 445941
	email:	
can of beer: $incl.		half day-
lime juice: $incl.		island hopping: 1 incl.
mineral water: $incl.		sunset fishing: 1 incl.
Dive centre		Gasfinolhu
	single dive, all equipment: $	
	five dives, all equipment: $	
	certified open water course: $	

GIRAVARU

Flying.....n/a
Speed boat.....15 mins
Dhoni.....45 mins

North Malé Atoll

〜 IF YOU ARE AIMING FOR A GOOD BEACH AND LAGOON ON a small island close to Male, this could be your target. It is well priced for its looks and facilities, though the cost of that is a lack of space *not* under roof or concrete.

Just a few minutes on a motorboat from the airport brings you to this empty south-west corner of Male' atoll. Dolphins pass by daily, a grey reef shark patrols near the jetty, a boat, having misjudged the reef, lies in the shallows. The diving, snorkeling and big game fishing is as good here as anywhere.

The sixty six rooms are evenly divided between the west side and the east side, with one two-storey block of twelve rooms between them on the narrow south side. A good beach stretches right around the three sides, kept in place by occasional, solid groynes. One beach (west) looks out over a large lagoon, ideal for watersports and diving lessons and sundowner drinks, of course. The other (east) is ideal for snorkeling, with its nearby reef drop off.

All the rooms are sold as the same and certainly it's only a couple of minutes from one side of the island to the other, but some rooms are not yet at the same maintainance standard as others, particularly in the bathroom. Not all rooms have a 'gifili' (open air) part to their bathroom, but all the other facilities are in common (satellite tv, telephone, minibar, hairdryer, jug of water). They are a decent size, well lit and pretty well decorated.

Round about half the guests are on full board and the other half are split evenly between half board and all-inclusives. For all-inclusives, all drinks, including premium spirits are free, but only up to midnight. Windsurfing and canoeing is in but excursions are not. Lunch is a set plate (good) and dinner is buffet. Every Saturday is a garden dinner for everyone and the occasional garden grill (excellent) is merely discounted for the full and half boarders. A lovely cafe, looking out past the jetty (to the dolphins if you're lucky), serves tastey fare all day.

Good beach, good lagoon, good value

Two thirds of the guests here are Italian, British are most of the remaining third, with Austrians, Russians and Dutch making up the remainder. Even though one of the two bars is closed after six, evenings don't really take off. This may be more to do with the tired resident band than the nationality mix. Whatever, the loyal senior staff and smiling barstaff and waiters are, you feel sure, doing the best they can.

It is not exactly clear where Giravaru is pitched in the market, but one thing is for sure, if you get a half decent price for your holiday here you'll enjoy it.

Resort	*tel*: 440440 *fax*: 444818
	email: giravaru@dhivehinet.net.mv
can of beer: $3.30	half day-
lime juice: $4.40	island hopping: $20
mineral water: $3.30	sunset fishing: $12
Dive centre	PlanetaDivers
	single dive, all equipment: $40
	five dives, all equipment: $220
	certified open water course: $484

Hakura Club

Flying.....40 mins
Speed boat.....n/a
Dhoni.....n/a

Meemu Atoll

〜〜 A SIMPLE, ALL-INCLUSIVE RESORT, HAKURAA CLUB HAS a number of good aspects but is let down by its geography. A large, very shallow lagoon means that it's a five hundred metre walk to the end of the jetty to reach water above waist height, and another four hundred metres to reach the house reef. Given that, the staff do an excellent job in minimising the problem and making the rest of your stay relaxing and hassle-free.

A dhoni is put on twice a day to take guests to the housereef and once a week there's a full-day snorkeling excursion. A regular free service to a reef-edge platform is planned. Snorkeling equipment is free and the fish life is good, but, as is the case everywhere, to see live corals you will have to go diving. Happily the dive school is friendly, small and well-equipped. Not only that, but as one of only two resorts on this new tourist atoll, the sites are untouched. A nearby channel provides several excellent dives for both novices and experts, though tilas and giris are the mainstay of the diving. For variety, you should enjoy the inter-atoll cargo shipwreck, with fridge-freezers still on board, which is ninety minutes away.

Dive and Sail, as the name suggests, run the watersports centre as well as the dive school. As part of the all-inclusive deal, the windsurfing is free, but canoes and catamarans have to be paid for. At anything approaching low tide watersports are impossible, but, water levels permitting, there are a few lovely uninhabited islands, strung out within the lagoon which are ideal for personal excursions.

Resort excursions are the usual round of fishing and island hopping. None are included in the package deal, but the local island visits should be good, as the islands are relatively unchanged by tourism.

In addition to the windsurfing and snorkelling equipment, the all-inclusive package means full board plus 'high tea' and free beverages. House wine is available only at lunch and dinner, and premium spirits are not included.

The food is excellent and varied. The

Relative price

8

8

Density of rooms to island size:

restaurant, bar and reception building is bright and spacious under its white, pavilion-like canopy. This odd, but appealing style of white, tent-like roofs appearing above the vegetation all over the island is reminiscent of the field camp of some medieval prince. It only lacks a few heraldic flags.

The seventy waterbungalows are linked together by one long boardwalk. Most face south to catch the sun, but, at one end, they face the sunrise only. They are larger inside than they appear from outside. This may be to do with the

simplicity of the furnishings and that the conical roof sits over a rectangular base. The heavy-duty pvc roof, though white, gives the a/c unit a fight to cool the place.

The bed is comfy and the bathroom is very decent. There are no windows in the walls, but sliding glass windows run the length of the side facing the water. It is private inside, but stepping outside you are in full view of neighbours on both sides. There are plans for screening trellises. In addition to the waterbungalows there are a few land

rooms officially for overbooking situations, but for some people preferable, as they are private and close to the beach.

The beach is not of the very finest sand, but it is broad and runs the length of one side of the island (the opposite side to the water bungalows). At one end is the bar/ restaurant building and at the other is a quiet bar and cafe.

The resort has a majority of Germans, with British, Italians, Japanese and French making up the remaining forty or so percent. As a well-serviced all-inclusive it is hassle-free, and being the first resort in the atoll brings its own advantages. It is just a shame it has perhaps the shallowest lagoon of any resort.

Resort	tel: 460014 fax: 460013
	email: hakura@dhivehinet.net.mv
can of beer: $3.30	half day-
lime juice: $4.40	island hopping: $20
mineral water: $3.30	sunset fishing: $10
Dive centre	Dive & Sail
	single dive, all equipment: $55
	five dives, all equipment: $275
	certified open water course: $460

HALAVELI

Flying......20 mins
Speed boat......n/a mins
Dhoni......n/a mins

Ari Atoll, north-east

∿ HALAVELI IS THE KIND OF RESORT YOU GO BACK TO

year after year. Encircling beaches of the finest white sand and first class diving are temptation enough, but not so rare in the Maldives. The real pull of this resort is the **atmosphere**. Built up over many years of an unchanging management and staff, the resort is truly welcoming, relaxing and fun.

It helps, of course, that the island is well endowed. A good **beach** runs all the way around this 'D' shaped island, extending at two points into huge tongues of pure sand. One of these extensions is in front of the bar, facing west, where many congregate each evening to watch the sun go down.

Generally speaking Halaveli is not as 'clubby' as many other Italian resorts. There is no animation during the day, as guests are encouraged to experience the real Maldives by getting into and under the water and by taking excursions. Indeed, one of the liveliest times of the day is when all the boats are heading off in the morning to go diving, snorkeling, fishing or on some island excursion.

For an Italian resort, **diving** is extremely popular here (as it is in the neighbouring, non-Italian resorts). one of the many good reasons for this is the three Protected Marine Areas close-by. One is renowned as the white tip reef shark capital of the Maldives, one is the grey reef shark capital and the third is unsurpassed for corals and the smaller reef fish. And since the dive centre is a five star instructor training centre, you know you are being well guided.

Relative price:

10

6

Density of rooms to island size:

The resort is truly welcoming, relaxing and fun

The fifty six **bungalows** (forty eight to I Grande Viaggi) are constructed in the raw Maldivian style of thatched roof and walls of unplastered coral and mortar; nearly all of them set back from the beach under the shade of tall coconut palms. Inside they are turn-of-the-century European, decorated in a comforting 'family house' style, with dark, carved wood, wallpaper, cornicing and subdued floral textiles. They have a telephone, minibar and air conditioning. The bathrooms are all modern, with lots of hot water and a good shower.

Around eighty percent of the guests here are Italian, with French and Japanese making up most of the rest. There are no specific facilities for children but the resort being as it is, children are accommodated happily. One bonus is that there is always a doctor on the island.

As for the main reception buildings on the resort, they are have a 'temporary' feel about them, neither very solid nor attractive. That, and the fact that the house reef is not great, are the two

failings of the resort. But these things are quickly forgotten as the guests are seduced by the ambience of the place, and in no time they are talking of coming back. In fact the staff come back as often as the guests, which really adds to the 'welcome back' feel and the smooth operation of this happy resort.

Resort	tel: 450559	fax: 450564
	email: halaveli@dhivehinet.net.mv	
can of beer: $2.75	half day-	
lime juice: $3.30	island hopping: $50	
mineral water: $3.30	sunset fishing: $20	
Dive centre		
	T.G.I.	
single dive, all equipment: $46		
six dives, all equipment: $276		
certified open water course: $420		

HELENGELI

Flying.....15 mins
Speed boat.....120 mins
Dhoni.....n/a

North Malé Atoll

〰 **THIS IS THE MOST ISOLATED RESORT IN MALÉ** atoll. And the people who come here love that because Helengeli is another big diving island. Run exclusively by Manta Reisen (but no longer under Swiss management), Swiss count for two thirds of the guests, with Germans, Austrians, Italians and British making up the rest.

Initially opened way back in 1979, the resort recently had a major refit and reopened in December 1996 (and was overbooked by Christmas). All the **rooms** were rebuilt with a/c and hot and cold fresh water, the bar and restaurant were extended and refurbished, and a brand new reception was added.

None of the buildings, however, can be seen from the shore line as there was very little extra cutting of this densely vegetated island. The birdlife bears witness to its natural state. One third of the place is unused. This is the eastern end open to the ocean and annually battered by the north-east monsoon. It is considered too dangerous to snorkel or dive on this side.

The north side of the island has fine **beaches**, the south side less so (and sometimes non-existent). This leads to some room changes but, on the other hand, there are no groynes here nor retaining walls or lagoon walls. The

lagoon is fairly small and full of coral so there is no watersports centre, but the snorkelling is wonderful. It is generally considered to be among the best **house reefs** in the Maldives.

Unaccompanied house reef **dives** are permitted throughout the day and into the evening. Indeed the dive centre staff have a fairly low profile as nearly all the divers here are advanced, many with hundreds of dives logged. There are few courses given for this reason. Instruction is on an ad hoc basis to bring the less experienced up to be able to deal with the conditions. Divers sign up for one boat and stick with it. In this way the instructor gets to know individuals and their standard, and the divers get to

know each other.

As this is an isolated island there is no competition for sites - there are, as they say, no bubble dives. Most of the dives are channel dives or thila dives, occasionally starting at twenty metres down

Relative price:

8

3

Density of
rooms to
island size:

*This resort is a mecca for the
advanced diver.*

looking underused. Guests prepare their kit half an hour before the dive and it is taken onto and off the boat for them. They can then take their time before coming back to wash and hang their stuff up in their personal cubicle.

As usual on dive islands excursions and evening activities are not a priority. As this place is out on its own the excursions are necessarily more expensive, but half and full-day snorkel and picnic trips are organised to the uninhabited island Kagi, and if ten passengers get together then a trip to the inhabited island of Gaafaru is also available. If you need a disco or late night drinking or other entertainments and competitions, then this resort is not for you. But if you want to dive, then you can do no better than come here.

and often with a considerable current. Exciting stuff, but not for the novice. A good example is Helengeli thila just fifty metres off shore. The top is at twelve metres and the current is sometimes treacherous, but, as Tim Godfrey in 'Dive Maldives' says, "for sheer abundance of marine life, Helengeli thila is hard to beat". He names a few of the big species: white tip reef shark, barracuda, tuna, trevally, black snapper and a resident 1.6 metre giant grouper. I can just add sighting a huge leatherback turtle in the deep sea approaching the resort.

The Ocean Pro dive centre is large, new and purpose-built, with all new equipment. Though about eighty bottles are filled a day the centre has the knack of

Resort	tel: 444615 fax: 442881
	email: engeli88@dhivehinet.net.mv
can of beer: $3.30	half day-
lime juice: $3.30	island hopping: $29
mineral water: $3.30	sunset fishing: $15
Dive centre	Ocean Pro
	single dive, all equipment: $44
	five dives, all equipment: $220
	certified open water course: $480

HILTON

Flying......35 mins
Speed boat......on request
Dhoni......n/a

Ari Atoll, south-west

⌒ HILTON HAVE NOW SUC-
CEEDED IN MAKING RANGALI
island their own. It took a couple of
years to turn the mediocre resort they
inherited into the first class place one
expects to find. Today it is a genuinely
classy resort and spa, a world away from
their renowned city hotels.

Indicative of the changes is the spa. First
there was none, then there was a Clarins
beauty treatment place, now there is a
real spa run by the renowned Raison d'Etre
company offering wonderful healing and
reinvigorating massages .

The cuisine is also wonderful now. Due to
the young Australian chef, Mark, you
won't find better food anywhere in the
country. The main dining room has a
Western section and an Eastern section.
Two nights a week are set menus,
including an innovative Maldivian night
on the ground around the pool. The
specialist restaurant is truly special.
Circular, open-sided and over the lagoon,
an evening of fine dining under the stars
will long stay in the memory. And
lunchtime snacks in the main bar are not
only good but reasonably priced too.

But don't think the options stop there.
Places experienced catering for the well-
off do not limit the possibilities to the
written schedules. There is a yacht
anchored offshore and if you wish you
can hire it for the evening and your meal
will be ferried out to you, course by
course. Or you may wish to have a
barbecue outside your room or at the
very end of the beach. Nothing is too
much trouble, it seems, for this conscien-
tious and committed management.

However, there is not too much anyone
can do about nature and the Hilton has a
couple of draw backs to do with the
lagoon. Two islands make up the resort
and the lagoon is very shallow on all but
one side, the east side of the main island

(looking into the atoll). It is only on this side too that the reef edge comes in near enough to snorkel. Still, the beaches are always broad and fine and, thanks to a successful planting programme there is also plenty of shade under the palms, at least on the main island.

A genuinely classy resort and spa.

Relative price

4

7

Density of rooms to island size:

The second island is linked by a foot-bridge and a ferry. It hasn't got many palm trees, there's no snorkeling to speak of and the lagoon is very shallow but it does have what some people travel the world over to find - true peace and quiet. There are just thirty water bungalows on the island and one other small thatched building that acts as a separate check-in, a lounge, breakfast room and snack bar. The water bungalows themselves are lovely: large, wooden and luxurious with extras such as a mini hi-fi, an espresso machine, complimentary water and a bath tub that looks out to the sun setting somewhere out over Africa.

The hundred beach bungalows on the main island are stylish too, in a modern minimalist fashion. Indeed the interiors of all the buildings are a delight. White paint, sunny textiles, coral, wood and sand on the floor combine a welcoming informality with expensive taste.

And yet this is not as expensive as some in the same top bracket. So enjoy!

Resort	*tel*: 450629	*fax*: 450619
	email:hilton@dhivehinet.net.mv	

can of beer: $4.00	full day-
lime juice: $3.00	island hopping: $65
mineral water: $4.00	sunset fishing: $15

Dive centre   Subaqua
single dive, all equipment: $66
six dives, all equipment: $294
certified open water course: $500

HOLIDAY ISLAND

Flying.....35 mins
Speed boat.....150 mins
Dhoni.....n/a mins

Ari Atoll, south

〰 **WHEN YOU LOOK AT WHAT THIS RESORT HAS TO OFFER** and compare the price you *can* pay for it, you must conclude that it is one of the best *value* for money resorts in the country. It is very large and doesn't look particularly 'Maldivian', but it has all the ticks in all the boxes, plus some, and the service is second to none.

All one hundred and forty two *rooms* are the same and are individual bungalows except for eighteen put together in pairs, with an adjoining door, for families. They are each spacious, well built and perfectly maintained. Top quality fixtures and fittings (from Singapore) are used throughout. There is a minibar, a hairdrier, a telephone in the room and the bathroom and a widescreen satellite television with big speakers. The bathroom has an open air part with a powerful hot shower duplicated in the inside bath. Unfortunately the single painting in the room is of dubious taste.

One door from the room opens to the beach and another opens onto the winding path that runs all the way around the inside of the island. Inside this paved path are carefully tended shrubs, flowers, palms and other fruiting

trees and everyday a group of women from neighbouring Maamigili are brought over to sweep the earth a pristine white.

One of the best value for money resorts in the Maldives

At the end of the paths, at opposite ends of the island, are the watersports centre and the dive centre. The *watersports* centre, comprehensively equipped (including parasailing) and enthusiastically run by a young team, is perfectly placed on a fine, wide beach with a sharply sloping lagoon. The *dive centre* has its own small jetty and is busy with three boats heading out twice a day. This is the most renowned region

Relative price:

6

9

Density of
rooms to
island size:

in the atoll for diving, with a wide array of different dives sure to please. The popularity sometimes means meeting up with other groups from neighbouring resorts or safari boats.

When the resort is full you are not going to get the **beach** to yourself either, but, on the other hand, you will never be cramped as the beach extends almost all the way around the island (some erosion in the north-east corner). The south facing beach is particularly good and, of course, has the sun all day. The north side is a series of small beaches between small, low groynes. The **lagoon** is too large for access from the beach but there are four trips a day to the reef edge and one a week further afield for snorkellers.

Other, free, exercise options include table tennis, volleyball, basketball, badminton, tennis and a gym - plus a sauna and

steam bath to finish. Then there is the fishing, night fishing and early morning trawler fishing (which is exercise or relaxation depending on how seriously you take it).

In the evening the **entertainments** continue. Twice a week there's karaoke and disco, once a week a live band, a crab race and a beach party. In the main bar drinks are served until the last person leaves. In addition to that is a twenty four hour room service.

This is not a resort for those searching for that quiet, natural Maldivian style (the vast, almost sterile, reception building will tell you this straightaway), but for action, fun, facilities and excellent service at a good price this resort is hard to beat. German and Swiss make up eighty percent of the clientele, with Italians another ten percent.

Resort   *tel*: 450011   *fax*: 450022
    email: holiday@dhivehinet.net.mv

can of beer: $2.95   half day-
lime juice: $4.00   island hopping: $33
mineral water: $2.75   sunset fishing: $28

Dive centre   Calypso
single dive, all equipment: $45
five dives, all equipment: $215
certified open water course: $399

IHURU

Flying.....n/a
Speed boat.....30 mins
Dhoni.....n/a

North Malé Atoll

〰 **IHURU IS A PICTURE POSTCARD RESORT WHICH IS** in sympathy with its surroundings. The philosophy here is environmental friendliness and **harmony**. The glory of the place is its fish and coral gardens.

The water in the rooms is solar heated, the electric bulbs are energy saving, the detergents are biodegradable and all the waste is carefully and considerately disposed of. Everyone who comes here is made aware of the good practice that is needed to preserve this perfect lagoon and reef formation.

The island and reef are two almost perfect circles, one inside the other. Apart from the cleared area around the jetty, the coral is abundant from a couple of metres away from the beach to the very edge, where it dramatically drops

straight down. Clearly this is among the very best **house reefs** in the country. Despite the past coral bleaching, snorkeling here is still a most rewarding pastime. The fish are still abundant.

Night diving the reef is another 'just walk in' treat. If you ever get tired of that, there are thirty five other sites within an hour's dhoni ride. Werner is now the dive base leader, having trained under the experienced, long-time base leader, Robert.

And then there's the **beach** - again, probably one of the best in the country for a small island. The policy here is not to build any walls or groynes into the sea. Which is admirable but does mean that the sand shifts around the island with each passing monsoon. The historical result of this seems to be an erosion of the north-east corner (beside the lagoon bar) and expansion of the south-west beach. To counter the full effects of this, sandbags are filled and covered over on the beach before the alternating seasons. This low-tech., watch and learn approach is typical of the island's long-time owner, Mujtaba, and must, in the years to come, produce the best results.

The forty five **rooms** are identical thatched, white bungalows placed close together around the island's perimeter. On each verandah is a charming traditional wooden 'swing joli' and, uncharmingly, two white plastic sun loungers. The rooms themselves, although not air conditioned, are cool enough, light and clean. Each has a telephone, fridge, safe and hairdryer. The shower room is also bright and clean; open-sided to a small enclosure of sand and greenery. There is plenty of hot water but the shower is not strong.

The **restaurant** looks a bit old fashioned, but the food can't be faulted. It is all full board with breakfast buffets, six lunch buffets and a single dinner buffet. The breakfasts are particularly good, with real coffee, muesli, yoghurt and fruit as well as a selection of fresh fruit

Relative price:

7

8

Density of rooms to island size:

Resort   *tel*: 443502   *fax*: 445933
       email: ihuru@dhivehinet.net.mv

can of beer: $3	full day-
lime juice: $3.50	island hopping: $35
mineral water: $3.25	sunset fishing: none

Dive centre   Dive Society
       single dive, all equipment: $50
       five dives, all equipment: $250
       certified open water course: $490

juices (e.g. passion fruit, grapefruit and mixed fruit).

*The island and reef
are two almost
perfect circles,
one inside the other.*

This is a very small island and guests are restricted to an area around the outside. It is also a quiet island, so if you need a lot of space for yourself or if you like to party into the night then Ihuru might not be for you. But for the mixed Europeans (mostly Italians and Swiss) and Japanese who come here, it is paradise.

KANDOOMA

Flying.....n/a
Speed boat.....35 mins
Dhoni.....150 mins

South Malé Atoll

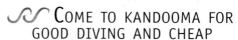 **COME TO KANDOOMA FOR GOOD DIVING AND CHEAP** accommodation. That is the common perception of this place, but recent major alterations have given it a significant face lift. Out of the lagoon has risen a new harbour for safari boats and a greatly enlarged beach that now boasts a swimming pool.

Every room has new furniture and a change of decor. There are one hundred and two rooms in all, either standard, beach superior and bungalows. Only the beach superiors and bungalows have a/c, but they all have fresh water. The standard rooms are small and still basic, the others are larger, lighter and quite smart. The thorough upgrading makes the whole place altogether more attractive.

It is the wonderful **diving** so close by that makes Kandooma worth considering.

No other island is quite this close to such a variety of grade one dives. (Not that it makes much difference between a five minute boat ride and twenty five, but there you are). On the edge of its own reef is "one of the underwater marvels of the Maldives", to quote the book 'Dive Maldives'. Kandooma Caves are probably the largest caverns in all the tourist atolls.

A couple of minutes down the channel is Kandooma thila. With its beautiful landscape and schools of trevally and bass, tuna and barracuda it is one of the best dives in the atoll. Then there is the vast Protected Marine Area called Guraidhoo Kandu on the opposite side of the island's reef. This is undoubtedly one of the best sites in the country. Your group may well not be alone, however, because there are eight other resorts in the neighbourhood.

Snorkelling is not feasible in the large, shallow **lagoon** so there are two trips out a day for the purpose, as well as a cheap special snorkelling trip to two nearby reefs. The lagoon at the front of the resort is almost enclosed by the large inhabited island just opposite so the water is slow moving and not the typical clear turquoise by any means.

At the front of the resort is a big, manufactured **beach**. It serves its purpose, though it is compacted and there isn't much shade. At the back (facing the ocean), the shore is all coral stone, large and small; terrific for tide pool enthusiasts, but not for sun bathers.

Breakfasts and lunches are set meals, dinners are buffet. The restau-

Relative price:

10

5

Density of rooms to island size:

rant is attractive and well lit, but the **food** is not up to the same standard. Outside the restaurant is a airy lounge corridor with arches, that curves around to the reception. Service at this point is so laid back as to be almost self-service. And that's fine, it suits the atmosphere of the place. There isn't much of a divide between the friendly staff and guests.

There is a camaraderie on this island and most people will enjoy it here, especially if you are German (nearly everybody *is* German), you dive and don't mind cheap food and accommodation.

Resort   *tel*: 444452   *fax*: 445948
             email: kandooma@dhivehinet.net.mv

can of beer: $2.42   full day-
lime juice: $3.85   island hopping: $25
mineral water: $2.20   sunset fishing: $15

Dive centre   Aquanaut
             single dive, all equipment: $55
             five dives, all equipment: $230
             certified open water course: $419

KANUHURAA

Flying......40 mins
Speed boat......n/a
Dhoni......n/a

Lhaviyani Atoll

⌇⌇ KANUHURA BEACH & SPA RESORT, TO GIVE IT

its full name, is a brand new addition to the top league. A wonderful blend of eastern and western cultures has resulted in a style and ambience that seduces and pampers, relaxes and reinvigorates.

Beautiful young men and women from Bali, Thailand, Philipinnes and other points East float around in sarongs smiling and serving in that uniquely deferential and calm manner. Behind them is a raft of European management evidently doing their job well.

The spa is a perfect example. The largest and most comprehensive facility in the country, it offers a wide selection of both eastern and western treatments. The masseuses are all Eastern, while the manager and director are Western (Australian). Combined with an interior design that exudes calm, an extraordinarily good fruit juice bar, health food menu, meditation and excercise spaces and you have the complete holiday spa experience.

As befitting the only resort with the word spa in its title, the building is in the centre of the public area, in front of the set-piece swimming pool. It could be, with every justification, the focus of your holiday, but it needn't be. Your preference might run more to cigars and cognac and so lead you to the surprising and surprisingly convincing Havana Lounge. Dimpled leather armchairs in a cool, dim setting, an upright piano and lady singer, knowledgeable staff and

humidity-controlled cabinets of fine cigars.

Then again, discos, pool and karaoke might be your thing and still Kanuhura scores well. For the sporty there's tennis and squash. And, of course, there is the watersports centre, perfectly sited on one tip of the island. The wind runs across the vaste, empty lagoon making catamaran and windsurfing conditions ideal.

But there's the rub. The same vaste, empty lagoon means no snorkeling. The dive centre, however, does its best to overcome this with several accompanied trips a week, including a wreck snorkel and night snorkeling. The diving itself is excellent. Llaviyani atoll is packed with channels, narrow and wide, attracting the big palagics and the full list of sharks. Although there are now three resorts in this corner of the atoll (and four resorts in the whole atoll) that still represents undisturbed diving.

Relative price:

3

4

Density of rooms to island size:

The beaches right around the island are terrific - wide, white and soft. On the other hand, there are very few palm trees around, and the rooms are half visible all the way down. But with tall bushes there is good privacy between the rooms.

The first resort with 'spa' in its name and deservedly so

The eighteen waterbungalows are fractionally wider than the eighty beach rooms, but otherwise the same, even to having (the only) open bathrooms over water. Interior design, materials and accessories are predictably top class, with incense, 'heliotherapy' lotions and robes reflecting the spa emphasis. In addition to these rooms there two waterbungalow suites and two extra special beach suites.

A small disappointment was the food, which may seem churlish as the menus are as varied as they are inventive, and, furthermore, their presentation is nothing short of beautiful, and yet nothing quite tasted as good as it looked or sounded. Still, that may change as this professional outfit constantly reviews and improves every human aspect of what is already a marvelous resort.

Resort	*tel*: 230044	*fax:* 230033
	email: kanuhura@kanuhura.com	
	can of beer: $2.42	full day-
	lime juice: $3.85	island hopping: $25
	mineral water: $2.20	sunset fishing: $15
Dive centre		Aquanaut
	single dive, all equipment: $61	
	five dives, all equipment: $243	
	certified open water course: $549+	

Komandoo

Flying.....40 mins
Speed boat.....4 hrs
Dhoni.....n/a

Lhaviyani Atoll

KOMANDOO IS THE QUIET, PRETTY AND TASTEFUL SISTER of its neighbour, the loud and self-confident Kuredu. Excursions are often merged with the much larger resort and the dive sites are shared, but otherwise the guests have very different Maldivian holiday experiences.

Komandoo has just forty five individual, wooden, beach-side bungalows. Constructed of Finnish pine, there is a distinctive Scandinavian feel to them. Modern and minimalist, they are also warm and luxurious. A discreet mini hifi system is typical of the thoughtful interior decor (there are around 250 cds to borrow from the reception). Enjoying the room is very much part of this resort experience, especially as each room steps down onto deep, soft sand with the lagoon just a few metres away.

The beach is perfect almost all around the island. Set back in a channel away from the outer ocean, the resort enjoys that ideal combination of wide beach, small lagoon and nearby reef. The beach is not untouched by efforts to keep all the beach in place all the year round, but, at least, they are discreet coral-bagging efforts.

Snorkeling around the island is still excellent. One marine biologist from Hamburg counted 265 species without ever going for a dive! Two of the bigger species taking regular short cuts through the channel are mantas and dolphins. Not that you have to go far for your diving, there are fifteen dive sites within fifteen minutes. Almost nowhere else in the tourism atolls do you have such a concentration of narrow channels one after the other, with their many corners, thilas and giris.

The dive base is as new as all the equipment, but the experience of the staff is gleened from many years on Kuredu. An underwater photography and

The quiet and tasteful sister of Kuredu

video course is a speciality here, along with other courses for nitrox, shark and ray dives, deep dives and drift dives.

It is somewhat of a surprise to have such an active dive scene on the island, when almost three quarters of the guests are on all-inclusive deals. It must really be tempting. Nearly everybody is either German or British, if they're not then they must be Italian or Swedish.

The pervading atmosphere is one of quiet. A place for people to relax and rejuvenate. Although it is so small the management can adapt quickly to different client groups, generally there is little in the way of evening entertainments.

The tall, swaying palms and the perfumed flowers found inside the island are idyllic. But the palms cut down around the outside expose the rooms to each other on the beach, at least for now. It is a lovely little resort set to get even lovelier.

Resort   tel: 231010   fax: 231011
            email: komandoo@dhivehinet.net.mv

  can of beer: $4   full day-
   lime juice: $3.25   island hopping: $24
mineral water: $2.50   sunset fishing: $25

Dive centre   Pro Divers
        single dive, all equipment: $49
        five dives, all equipment: $235
        certified open water course: $548

Relative price:

5

8

Density of rooms to island size:

KUDAHITHI

∿ **KUDAHITHI IS NOT SO MUCH** a resort as a house with seven exotic rooms. A quiet, peaceful house on a tiny island surrounded by a coral garden.

Kuda means **small** and this island takes less than ten minutes to walk around. Apart from the rooms (and a small service area) there is only one other building. Walking off the jetty one steps into the parlour of some turn-of-the-century bourgeois country house. Here is the heavy black wooden furniture, the tapestry cushions, the solid display cabinets and the samovar. As it only has three sides it is like a stage set looking out not to an audience but to the Indian Ocean.

The seven **rooms** are stage sets too, for your own private **fantasie**s. Choose from The Sheikh Room, The Captain Room, The Rehendi Room (Maldivian queen), The Safari Room, The Maldives Room,

The Bali Room and The Maharaja Room. Yes it's kitsch, but it is lavish, Italian designed kitsch. And never cheap. The spears in the safari room are original Masai weapons; the leopard spot floor tiles are by Krizia; other tiles are by Versace and Valentino; the bathroom of The Captain Room has cork tiling from Sardinia. In addition to the expected facilities (though no hairdryer or minibar), each room has a video, to play any of the seventy odd videos held by the manager.

There isn't a **beach** all the way around the island. One side has a wall at the shoreline, but the three rooms on this side are compensated with a wooden sun deck that stretches up to and over the wall and has steps down to the shallows. The other four rooms have a fine wide beach in front of them. And surrounding the whole island is a wonderful coral garden. The coral is so dense and close to the surface that you must go off one of the two jetties to reach the reef edge.

Diving is free and if anybody wishes to go the dive boat from Boduhithi will stop by on the way out to pick them up. For watersports one must take the five minute boat ride over to that island. That too is free, but most guests seem to be happy lazing out in the 'garden' or sipping coffee in the 'house'.

Relative price:

Density of
rooms to
island size:

The **food** is entirely Italian, with the accent on fresh fish. Breakfast and lunch are buffet and dinner is served at your table. Every day there are two types of pasta, one white and one red, but you can stay here for fifteen days and never repeat a dish. With so few other guests and such a fine setting, dining is a distinctly civilized pleasure. A rather English touch is the tea and cake served every day at four o'clock.

This is a very **quiet**, private island. There is no music and there are no activities except board games. It is a beautiful place to do nothing.

Resort   tel: 444613   fax: 441992
        email: hcmmale@clubvacanze.com.mv

can of beer: incl.   half day-
lime juice: incl.   island hopping: incl.
mineral water: incl.   sunset fishing: incl.

Dive centre   Boduhithi
              single dive, all equipment: $incl.
              five dives, all equipment: $incl.
      certified open water course: $400

KUDARAH

Flying.....25 mins + 30 dhoni
Speed boat.....120 mins
Dhoni.....n/a

Ari Atoll, south-east

∿ KUDARAH IS ANOTHER RESORT RUN ENTIRELY BY

Club Vacanza. It is smaller than the others (apart from Kudahithi), more Mediterranean in appearance, more expensive and a little more formal.

If you didn't look at the palm trees or turquoise water you might well imagine yourself in some European destination, a real home from home for Italian sun-seekers. The buildings have balustrades, arches, terracotta tiles over verandas,

and flat roofs. Inside, all is white and spacious, with antiques and objets d'art.

This elegance is echoed in the landscape. Fortunate to have a mature island with tall palms and a full canopy, it has been enhanced with bowers of bougainvilia, frangipani trees and flowers.

Unfortunately the island has not been well endowed with **beaches**. During the high season there is really only one beach, near the jetty, and that looks out to a prominent lagoon wall not far away. Still, this doesn't seem to disturb people here, as the guests enjoy coming together in one place, and the walls create the effect of a large swimming pool, ideal for communing. In the later afternoon when shadows fall across this spot everyone, it seems, takes the short dhoni ride over to a glorious, pure sandbank to continue the tanning and playing. At other times of the year the beach is well spread around the island.

Outside the walls the reef edge is excellent for *snorkeling* and this is

Relative price:

4

8

Density of
rooms to
island size:

*A Mediterranean style resort
in a Maldivian setting*

There are just thirty, well-appointed,
rooms on this small island so, with the
help of the friendly and attentive staff, a
camaraderie is quickly formed, and with
it a memorable holiday.

Resort	tel: 450610	fax: 450550
	email: hcmmale@clubvacanze.com.mv	
can of beer: incl.		half day-
lime juice: incl.		island hopping: incl.
mineral water: incl.		sunset fishing: incl.
Dive centre		Kuda Rah
	single dive, all equipment: $ incl.	
	five dives, all equipment: $ incl.	
	certified open water course: $ 400	

indeed popular, but diving is not taken
up by many here despite some fine dive
sites close-by. There are a few canoes for
general use but no actual watersports
centre. The activities are more land
based. In the middle of the island is one
of the few really good **tennis courts**.
Volleyball is also available. So too is
pool, table tennis and darts.

Entertainment is similar to that found
on other Italian resorts, though perhaps
less participatory here. Every evening
there is a small cabaret, and after lunch
with coffee and before dinner with
aperitifs members of staff put on a
performance of familiar songs.

One of the highlights of the resort is the
food. Lunch is a large and varied buffet
washed down with the carafes of ice tea
and white wine provided, and rounded
off with home-made ice cream. Guests
dress up for dinner as it were to do
justice to the five excellent courses
served at the table. The enjoyment is
audible in the chatter and laughter
around the dining room.

KURAMATHI

Flying.....15 mins
Speed boat.....105 mins
Dhoni.....n/a

Rasdhoo Atoll

Three res...
Kuramathi has...

〰️ **UNIQUELY, THIS ISLAND HAS THREE SEPARATE HOTELS** on it, although all of them are owned and run by the same company. The standard 'Village' occupies the eastern end, the up-market 'Cottage' is in the middle and the slightly less up-market 'Blue Lagoon' is on the western tip.

Guests are free to move about between the resorts (a bus runs up and down all day) to try out the other restaurants and bars, the varied nightlife or simply to explore. Every night there is some live band, disco or beach party at one or other resort. The whole island is most attractively landscaped and the low, thatched buildings fit handsomely into the environment. The three resorts are, nonetheless, quite clearly graded.

The standard of interior design and the materials used inside the **Village** bar, restaurant and rooms is moderate, but that is why it is cheaper. The **bar** is an unpretentious, lively place that tends to stay open later than those of the other hotels. A pertinent reason for this is that about eighty percent of the guests here are on **all-inclusive** deals. On Kuramathi that covers a range of premium brand drinks (125 cocktails), snacks, one excursion and one fishing trip.

The **restaurant** is ordinary looking, and so is the food. This is a good reason (and this may not be accidental) to try out the **alternative restaurants**. At the Village this is the Adoobe Grill serving fine meat, fish and seafood on the beach. There is a five percent discount for those on half and full board.

The one hundred and forty four **rooms** range from the basic block rooms (seventy) to the larger, lighter round bungalows (forty four) and onto the well appointed, shady and cosy wooden bungalows (thirty). The all newly rebuilt block rooms have the advantage of being closer to the bar and restaurant and the good **beach**. The other rooms are on a quiet part of the island, but the beach pretty much disappears at high tide.

The **Cottage** has fifty **water bungalows** all in a row, and thirty three beach

Relative price:

8+5

6

Density of
rooms to
island size:

ne island,

ng for everyone.

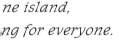

bungalows. The water bungalows are the best rooms on the island (and are exactly the same as those on Baros), with good textiles and excellent fixtures and fittings, a minibar, telephone, bedside radio and a verandah on three sides with steps down to the lagoon. A short swim away is a fine, long reef. The beach rooms are cozy but don't have a beach.

There is a man-made beach behind the bungalows which is not too bad, but the main beach is on the other (inside atoll) side, where the **watersports** centre for all three hotels is sited (and the tennis court). The bar, restaurant and lounge building of the Cottage is exclusive looking and, especially in the evening with thoughtful lighting in and around the place, it is particularly conducive to relaxed drinking and dancing. The two speciality restaurants are a Thai and the Palm Court Grill.

The **Blue Lagoon** is recognised as the quietest of the three, attracting families and a less young crowd. It is also the smallest, with just twenty water bungalows and thirty beach **rooms**. The bungalows have been redecorated to a high standard, while the beach rooms are plain but comfortable and well built. The bar, restaurant and lounge area is compact and comfortable, with a pleasant sundeck. At sunset guests gather here to watch the feeding of sting rays.

Outside the beach rooms is the longest stretch of open sand on the island, but the price to pay for this is a prominent sea wall. And at the very western tip is a lip of sand where romantics gather each day to watch the sun go down.

Resort	*tel*: 450527	*fax*: 450556
	email: sales@unisurf.com	

can of beer: $3.00	full day-
lime juice: $3.85	island hopping: $35
mineral water: $3.63	sunset fishing: $15

Dive centre Island Atoll & Rasdhoo Atoll
single dive, all equipment: $44
five dives, all equipment: $205
certified open water course: $450

Each resort has its own **dive centre** and the real prize here is the nearby **hammerhead shark** site. Here too is a large decompression chamber and mini-hospital run in conjunction with Halle University.

KUREDU

Flying.....40 mins
Speed boat.....240 mins
Dhoni.....n/a

Lhaviyani Atoll

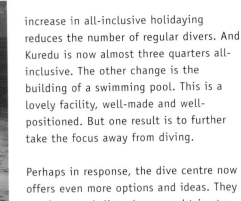

*It's a barefoot, lots-to-do,
come-and-party sort of resort.*

KUREDU IS NO LONGER THE LARGEST RESORT IN THE country, Sun Island takes that position, but it is still the liveliest. It is still the number one barefoot, lots-to-do, come-and-party place.

At one time this was a hardcore divers island, but a couple of recent changes have further reduced this bias. That is not to say this isn't a great place to dive from, it most certainly is. It is always the case, however, that the introduction or increase in all-inclusive holidaying reduces the number of regular divers. And Kuredu is now almost three quarters all-inclusive. The other change is the building of a swimming pool. This is a lovely facility, well-made and well-positioned. But one result is to further take the focus away from diving.

Perhaps in response, the dive centre now offers even more options and ideas. They run free snorkeling classes and trips to local sites for photo-snorkeling and shipwreck-snorkeling. Nitrox diving has been added to all the diving options and housereef diving with a buddy is just a matter of signing up and going. Plus the centre has had a refit to keep it looking and runnning as good as anywhere in the country. The dive sites around (particularly the channels and corners) have long been some of the best in the country.

The staff of the centre, like the staff throughout the resort, are happy and helpful. It is a positive aspect of a big resort that the staff cameraderie is strong and it pervades the island. Two excellent, outgoing animators also play a big part in giving the place a buzz. Some fun activity is set for every evening and the nights are given over to bar games, music quizzes, drinking and discoing. The number of discos is flexible, depending on the wishes of the guests that week.

The watersports centre here is also one of the few really active such places. Right on the main beach, it has thirty windsurf boards and six catamarans, plus a variety of canoe types. Among several island options is one ideal desert island with good snorkeling. And between five and six every evening dolphins are often seen (mantas even, occasionally) taking an atoll short-cut.

Of the three hundred rooms, three quarters are now superior and one quarter

Relative price:

9

4

Density of
rooms to
island size:

standard. All the rooms have had recent work done on them and they are now very satisfactory. Hot water in the shower, a/c and a fridge are the only differences between the categories. Other than the fact that the standards are at the 'back' of the resort, furthest away from the central public buildings, and they mostly have the least good beaches.

The beach along the front, protected from the open sea, is one long, wide strip of glorious off-white sand. At the back, it is partly protected by a sea wall, keeping some sections of good beach. At both ends of the island are further bulbs of sand, with a bar on each; one for sunset and one for sunrise (well, it is an all-inclusive ;))

My only real quibble with the place is the food. It may have improved some, but it is still not enticing. And this may be for

a reason. There are four very good food outlets apart from the main restaurant and there is no discount for any meals taken in them. The Maldivian Tea House is a most surprising and authentic touch. The Grill is cozy and romantic. Next door is a decent Far East/Thai place. And Franco's pizza and burger joint is hard to resist, with its al fresco aromas next to the swimming pool.

The clientele are a jolly mix of British, Germans, Italians, Swiss, Austrians, French and Swedish.

Resort	*tel*: 230337	*fax*: 230332
	email: info@kuredu.com	
can of beer: $3.25	half day-	
lime juice: $3.00	island hopping: $25	
mineral water: $2.50	sunset fishing: $15	
Dive centre	ProDivers	
	single dive, all equipment: $35	
	five dives, all equipment: $168	
	certified open water course: $495	

KURUMBA

Flying......n/a
Speed boat......8 mins
Dhoni......20 mins

North Malé Atoll

∾ **THE FIRST RESORT IN THE COUNTRY TO BE OPENED AND** the nearest to the airport, Kurumba leads a dual life. At one and the same time it is a holiday resort and a regular hotel.

The obvious choice for businessmen and visiting VIPs, it also suits holiday-makers who enjoy being in an environment of *luxury* and *service*. Now this probably includes all of us, but the reality is that you get less of a sense of the real Maldives here than usual. The focus of the resort is as much inward to the swimming pools, restaurants and bars as it is outward to the beach and lagoon.

No other island is as fully *landscaped* as this one. It is like one large garden, with colourful flowers (from tiny border plants to bowers of bougainvilia) and trimmed hedges under a canopy of tall coconut palms. Around about you will find the five restaurants, the coffee shop and the pizza outlet. The speciality restaurants are a Chinese, a French, an Indian and a Grill. Their reputation could be higher.

The largest *swimming pool* is a lovely creation centrally placed in front of the open-sided main bar. This, in many ways, is the hub of the resort. Tucked away in the interior is the second pool, within the sports centre, which also has two tennis courts, a gym, sauna and snooker table. An innovative spa has quickly gained a good reputation.

Of the one hundred and eighty *rooms* in total, there are eight suites, of which four are 'presidential' and four are 'junior'. These are lovely large rooms built and fitted to a high standard and carpeted throughout. The other rooms are deluxe; pleasantly decorated and well fitted-out. But with so many to fit onto a small island they are smaller than might be expected.

Outside every room is the welcome shade of tall palms and beyond that, the *beach*. It is a good beach all around the island, giving a choice of wide open stretches and little private areas between bushes. In a few areas unsightly old groynes

Relative price:

7

7

Density of
rooms to
island size:

extend from the shore, but more unsightly
is the wall of coral built inside the reef
edge all the way around. The best that
can be said of this, is that after a while
you no longer notice it.

Despite its proximity to Malé and its
outer harbour the water is still wonderfully clear and the *reef* edge still offers
excellent snorkelling. *Diving* too is very
good as the sites in South Malé Atoll are
accessible, as well as the roster of well-
known sites in this part of North Malé.

Kurumba is a convenient, cosmopolitan
resort which is meticulously tended and
maintained. The uniformed staff add to a
certain formality that exists here. It's
ideal for those who want a resort near
the airport with all the facilities and isn't
a barefoot and sand on the floor place.

Resort	*tel*: 442324 *fax*: 443885
	email:kurumba@dhivehinet.net.mv

can of beer: $3.40	half day-
lime juice: $5.50	island hopping: $23
mineral water: $4.40	sunset fishing: $25

Dive centre	Euro Divers
	single dive, all equipment: $49
	five dives, all equipment: $230
	certified open water course: $450

LAGUNA BEACH

Flying.....n/a
Speed boat.....20 mins
Dhoni.....55 mins

South Malé Atoll

∿ LAGUNA BEACH IS A HANDSOME LOOKING RESORT

close to Malé. Developed originally as an up-market resort, it is less expensive now without having lost any of its good looks, service or facilities.

In some ways there is a mix of people and what they want from their holiday. On the one hand are somewhat older, richer guests who enjoy peace and quiet, beautiful surroundings and a variety of restaurants. On the other hand are younger couples looking for a more active holiday: watersports and evening entertainments, possibly with child care.

The resort has so far managed wonderfully in catering to both sets of clients. Almost every night there is a live band, disco or other entertainment on in the main bar, by the swimming pool. Alterna-

tively, a quiet, romantic night could be had in one of the three specialist restaurants or on the verandah of your room, surrounded by flowers and far from any noise. It would be fair to say, however, that there is a general move towards a more lively, family-oriented set-up.

The buildings and the interiors belong to the grand, formal style of city hotels (like Kurumba and Full Moon Beach) which may or may not be to your taste. Like those resorts too, the rooms are close together but divided by, sometimes almost hidden behind, a colourful array of perfectly kept flowers and shrubs.

Fifty rooms are in two-storey blocks (four rooms per block), which include one suite of two rooms and one of three. Sixty five rooms are individual bungalows, which

are a little larger but otherwise similarly decorated to the regular block rooms. A third bed can be fitted in for children (cots are available too). A nice touch is the tea and coffee making facility (though the minibars are expensive). The new water bungalows are the finest rooms with good swimming and snorkeling.

There is a good variety of beachscape here, sometimes broad, sometimes small and private. There is also little in the way of groynes and walls, which makes it a pleasure to look at and walk around. The snorkelling is fair in the lagoon, but going out to the drop-off, although it is superb, is not recommended for novices because of the two often fast-flowing channels at the edge of the reef. Diving in the region is good, with the sites in

the southern part of North Malé also accessible.

A full list of tours is organised, including snorkelling excursions, Malé excursions, photo flights, glass-bottomed boat trips and all types of fishing. It used to be that these events were not well taken up, but with the changing clientele this resort is becoming a more 'happening', fun and family place.

Resort	tel: 445906 fax: 443041
	email: sales@unisurf.com
can of beer: $4.40	full day-
lime juice: $4.40	island hopping: $44
mineral water: $4.40	sunset fishing: $22
Dive centre	Euro Divers
	single dive, all equipment: $37
	five dives, all equipment: $220
	certified open water course: $450

LILY BEACH

Flying......25 mins
Speed boat......n/a
Dhoni......n/a

Ari Atoll, south-east

∿ LILY BEACH IS AN ALL-INCLUSIVE RESORT THAT successfully mixes the smart with the informal to give its guests a happy taste of the good life for the extent of their holiday.

It is *not* the cosy, thatched look of so many resorts, but the imposing, high-ceilinged appearance of a city hotel. In truth rather 'blocky' and dominated by a green on green colour scheme, yet made more informal by sand on the floor and low, comfy chairs. And by the easy-going attitude of guests and staff alike.

In this impressive setting everything is free, as it is all-inclusive (that is to say, you have already paid for it). All three meals are generous *buffets*, and there is a coffee shop if you get peckish in-between meals. In addition to food and drink at any time (but not the minibar), the quality tennis court and gym are free, as is the snorkelling and windsurfing equipment. However, only one half-day trip to a local inhabited island is also included.

The ninety four *rooms* are divided into superior (seventy eight), water bungalow (sixteen) and one deluxe suite. All the rooms are well-built and well-decorated with a pleasing attention to detail. The water bungalows are considerably bigger and have the addition of a hairdryer, bath and larger shower. All the fixtures and fittings are first class.

Relative price:

7

9

Density of
rooms to
island size:

*In this impressive setting
everything is 'free'.*

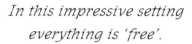

These water bungalows (which are actually over the edge of the narrow beach) face south, so they have the sun all day and they are just ten metres from the reef drop-off and excellent **snorkeling**. As I approached the island the blue water ahead turned a rippling green with a vast school of yellow-coloured, blue-striped snapper.

Diving in the region (not forgetting the superb house reef) is, as usual, very good but it is not as popular here as might be expected, because of the all-inclusive package. The professional and experienced Ocean Pro run the base.

As for **beaches**, there is a large bulb of sand on both ends of the island, one outside the swimming pool and bar and the other away on its own. In between, on the side with most of the rooms, the beach is long, fine and uninterrupted by any groynes, although there is a low wall in the lagoon all the way down. Unfortunately, this side faces north, north-west so the sun leaves it well before the end of the day.

Still, the resort overall is a bright, light place and the large, pastel-coloured buildings accentuate this. The service is very good, with the same attention to

detail noticable throughout the resort. A hassle-free holiday is assured.

The all-inclusive package comes at a price other resorts ask for bed and breakfast only, so you certainly get value for money.

Resort	tel: 450013	fax: 450646
	email: lilybech@dhivehinet.net.mv	

can of beer: incl.	half day-
lime juice: incl.	island hopping: incl.
mineral water: incl.	sunset fishing: $15

Dive centre   Ocean Pro
single dive, all equipment: $44
six dives, all equipment: $264
certified open water course: $480

LOHIFUSHI

LOHIFUSHI AS AN ISLAND IS LARGE, MATURE AND RICH

in coconut palms and other native trees, flowers and shrubs. It began as a resort in 1980 with just thirty standard rooms and now it has one hundred and twenty seven in four different categories. But what has really changed the place is the complete rebuilding of the public area in 1996 - the reception, bar, lounge, swimming pool, patio and so on.

The **rebuild**, in my opinion, has not been a success, and the resort is happy and friendly despite it rather than because of it. From outside, the odd decorative elements (pillars, chains and low posts) and the colour scheme of light blue and lime green give the place a birthday cake look. The interior has an appearance of grandeur which is not reflected in the quality of materials used. And then there are a few practical design problems such as the bar, which is in two parts around a very elevated, almost separate, dance floor. The outcome is a bar that is hard to get buzzing in the evening and a disco that doesn't 'take off'.

That said, the rest of the **island** is attractive. The large area in the middle is a green park under the shade of coconut palms. That in itself is rare for resorts, which are often too small to have an 'inside', or else it is cut off from guests and used for staff only. Walks along well-tended paths with water views take guests to their bungalows.

The impression of a semi-exclusive marina is accentuated by the modern complex of tennis, badminton, volleyball and squash

courts. The separate **sports** centre, out
on its own, is not well used but offers
weight-lifting and keep-fit equipment as
well as table tennis, pool, table-football
and board games. (It should all be in or
near the bar/lounge).

*A large, green resort whose
strength is its natural beauty*

The one hundred and twenty seven **rooms**
are categorised into standard, superior (the
majority of rooms), deluxe, suite and VIP
villa. The standard are divided into a/c
and non a/c, and both are just fine:
clean, white and unpretentious. The
other categories are differentiated by a
range of mostly unnecessary additions,
such as a small carpet, a towel rack, a
hairdryer and tiles below the sink. And
frankly, the suites are downright tacky
(pink rococo fittings).

The standard rooms are on the west side,
looking into the atoll, where the best
beach is (although divided by many
groynes). The deluxe (and family superior) are on the north-west and north

side where there is a fine spur of sand.
And the superior rooms are on the east
side where the beach is mostly coral with
sandy strips in-between. There is also a
low island wall here which is not too
unattractive.

Snorkeling is poor as the **lagoon** is huge
and shallow. Diving is good and popular,
though not the most modern set up I
have seen. **Watersports** are conveniently
placed and well run by a lovely, friendly
couple offering a good array of sports
and lessons. Surfing takes place on the
deserted southern end of the island by a
solid, but friendly, clique of older than
expected Australians.

Food is plain but satisfactory. Breakfast
and dinner are buffet, lunch is set. A
coffee shop is set beside the water's edge.

Three quarters of the guests here are
Germans and the remainder are an equal
mix of Austrians, English, Australians,
Japanese and Italians.

Resort	tel: 441909 fax: 441908
	email: lohifush@dhivehinet.net.mv

can of beer: $3.30	full day-
lime juice: $3.30	island hopping: $30
mineral water: $2.75	sunset fishing: $15

Dive centre Lohifushi
single dive, all equipment: $40
five dives, all equipment: $180
certified open water course: $290+

MAAFUSHIVARU

Flying......n/a
Speed boat......150 mins
Dhoni......4-6 hours

Ari Atoll, south-east

MAAFUSHIVARU IS A SMALL, PRETTY ITALIAN resort that can be booked only through **Turisanda**. Though it is well promoted by the company, almost all the rooms are taken by repeaters and those that have had personal recommendations. And that is always a good sign. The downside, for some, might be the modern, 'built' environment (e.g. tiled roofs and floors).

Although there are just thirty eight **rooms**, they are close together because the island is so small. On the other hand, the rooms themselves are large and spacious. And unlike many 'boxes', they are pleasingly designed, with angled walls and alcoves. As well as a/c, each room has a minibar, hairdryer and telephone. The shower rooms are a little on the small side and hot water is not available in the hand basins.

The ten water bungalows are inevitably more boxy and not as big, but they have a small, private verandah and steps down to the lagoon. There is no snorkelling just here, but the six facing east are not far from the reef edge. The four facing west have the sunset.

Set in an idyllic circular **reef**, the coral and fish life are **superb**. And further to local snorkelling there are organised trips to other great neighbouring reefs. **Diving** too is excellent, though there is actually not a big take-up (so your boat won't be full). Night fishing, morning trawler fishing and big game fishing are other items on the full **excursion** programme. There is also a full-time aerobics and water aerobics leader, though it is probably true to say that this resort is less active or 'clubby' than many other Italian resorts.

Almost all the rooms are taken by repeaters and those that have had personal recommendations.

There is a theatre but it is not used every night, there aren't musical entertainments after lunch and even beach volleyball isn't a daily event. Still, the atmosphere is close and friendly and much of the life is on the excellent **beach** which is broad, white and fine for most of the way around the whole island. There are prominent walls in the lagoon, but these are mostly outside the reception area rather than outside the rooms, so the views are not badly disrupted. The interior is attractively laid out and looked after, with many palms, clean swept sand

Relative price:

6

10

Density of
rooms to
island size:

paths and bowers of pink bougainvilia overhead.

All the meals are **buffets** and there is afternoon tea laid on as well (so there is no call for a coffee shop). The restaurant and reception area is styled somewhat like a 'summer pavilion', all pillars and trestles and pastel colours.

Overall this is a well-designed, if not exactly natural looking, small resort with

a very good beach and reef, targeted at the 'beautiful people'.

Resort	tel: 450596	fax: 450524
	email: sales@unisurf.com	
can of beer: $2.75		half day-
lime juice: $3.30		island hopping: $25
mineral water: $3.30		sunset fishing: $20
Dive centre		Sea Dragon
	single dive, all equipment: $50	
	ten dives, all equipment: $470	
	certified open water course: $500	

MACHCHAFUSHI

Flying......30 mins
Speed boat......n/a
Dhoni......n/a

Ari Atoll, south-east

〰 ESSENTIALLY, THIS IS A GERMAN-SPEAKING DIVE island, and as such it is excellent. With up to eighty percent of guests diving, the rhythm of the resort naturally reflects the rhythm of the divers' day.

Within easy reach are all the famed channels of south-east Ari Atoll. A whole series of thilas here (irregular columns of coral rising from the sea bed) offer an inexhaustible array of rewarding dives. All the main pelagics are here, as well as rare groups of soft and hard coral. And just inside the atoll is the Protected Marine Area, Kudahrah Thila, with its concentration of all these features. A site not to be missed.

The dive school (the German company Subaqua) is very efficiently, yet flexibly, run (apart from the exact time the boats leave). Escorted and unescorted house reef dives are possible at any time of day.

These are tremendously popular because the house reef is one of the best in the atoll (other resort guests often come over to snorkel it).

As divers often tire in the evening and want to be in shape for the morning dive, there isn't too much organized in the way of evening entertainments (one disco and one fire limbo with barbecue per week). The main bar, is, nonetheless, large and fully stocked. Under the same roof is a table tennis table, a dance floor and the restaurant. In the centre of the island is a good tennis court and a sand volleyball court. The windsurf centre is pretty well stocked but not greatly used, partly because the lagoon is small and the coral comes in close to shore most of the way around the island.

Although there aren't many coconut palms, there is a great deal of pleasant shade around the island, which has been

Relative price:

8

8

Density of
rooms to
island size:

particularly good shade between the rooms and the beach, so, with their thatched roofs, they are not even visible from the water.

Of the fifty eight rooms forty eight are called deluxe and ten are water bungalows. The deluxe rooms are large and well furnished, with a big double bed and solid, comfortable seating. There is a/c, h/c water, telephone and (unfilled) minibar. The single painting, though, is ugly. And the shower fixture could certainly be better. The water bungalows are similar to the deluxe rooms, but with the addition of satellite televisions.

The water bungalows also have individual balconies with steps down to a wonderful coral garden. They are sensibly built off the south side of the island where there really isn't a beach to talk of. Here there is an uprising of volcanic rock just off shore. For the rest of the island the beach varies from good to very good, with an excellent wide,

clean beach on the northern curve (though that means the sun is not shining in it for many hours)

A well placed coffee shop here serves snacks and drinks, though everyone is on full board. Drinks are inexpensive. Breakfasts and lunches are buffet and good, dinners are set plates (apart from one Asian buffet) and OK.

The rhythm of the resort naturally reflects the rhythm of the divers' day.

Three quarters of the guests are German or Austrian, with Japanese and Italians making up most of the rest, plus a few British and Australians. Snorkeling and tanning on the beach are fine, but you may feel a bit out of it if you don't actually dive, because that is really the preoccupation of the place.

left in a fairly natural state. Ironically, it is the areas that have been 'land-scaped' that look a bit shoddy. There is

Resort	*tel*: 454545	*fax*: 454546
	email:	
	can of beer: $2.42	half day-
	lime juice: $3.30	island hopping: $20
	mineral water: $2.75	sunset fishing: $16
Dive centre		Delphis
	single dive, all equipment: $49	
	six dives, all equipment: $294	
	certified open water course: $465	

MADOOGALI

Flying......20 mins
Speed boat......120 mins
Dhoni......n/a

Ari Atoll, north-west

MADOOGALI IS A GEM OF A RESORT, A MODEL FOR ANY other island. Few resorts are in such a natural state yet also completely up-to-date and stylish. Its secret is constant *maintenance* and a deep commitment to the *environment*.

Opened in 1989 it still looks brand new. The buildings are tastefully designed and kept in perfect order. Yet that, in some ways, is the easy part. Over time most resorts cannot resist the pressure to build groynes on the beach and walls in the lagoon in a never ending attempt to keep all the beaches in place throughout the year.

Madoogali has no groynes and no walls. The beach goes almost all the way around the island, and if it is not always wide that is a small price to pay. (It should be said that, unlike Madoogali, islands on the outside of atolls have to deal with big swells from the open sea landing directly on the shore).

A sandy path winds in front of the bungalows, shaded by mature palms, bowers of bougainvilia and native trees. Two paths cut across the island and in the middle where they meet is a garden. Here it is swept clean, otherwise leaves are left under the foliage to form compost. The whole effect is of a very well kept inhabited island. With the addition of delightful 'found' objects, such as driftwood, placed as sculptures.

> *Few resorts are so
> natural and
> so stylish*

The fifty individual **bungalows** are solidly constructed of coral and handsomely decorated inside and out. Large and well laid out, they include a telephone, a/c, h/c water and minibar. The shop, restaurant, bar and reception are sensibly joined together in one area.

The former manager, Georgio Lagorio (now in Bolifushi), left a legacy of concern for the environment. He instigated a number of environmentally-friendly procedures, such as sorting and disposing of all refuse in the most appropriate manner and recycling whatever is possible (for example, coconut husks and oil drums to local islanders, and kitchen waste turned into fertiliser).

Relative price:

7

5

Density of rooms to island size:

The new manager is the equally experienced and commited Mauricio Ciorra who recently spent more than six years as manager of Halaveli. Under his management the pulse of the resort has increased. Now there is a beach bar and disco and a full-on evening animation programme. The beach centre has also been improved with the addition of catamarans, windsurfers and pedalos.

The **reef** and lagoon are manually cleaned twice a month and are still good for snorkeling. There are also many, popular snorkeling excursions. The **dive centre** is a five star PADI centre and is lucky in having a good number of nearby sites pretty much to itself. Encouraging people to get off the island during the day, there is an inventive schedule of **excursions**, which includes their own neighbouring desert island, Vihaamaafaru.

Enjoying this top ranking resort, and consistently returning to it, are a majority of Italians (three quarters) with a significant number of French and Austrians, plus a few Germans.

Resort	tel: 450581	fax: 450554
	email: madugali@dhivehinet.net.mv	

can of beer: $3.50	half day-
lime juice: $2.50	island hopping: $12
mineral water: $3.50	sunset fishing: $12

Dive centre   Madoogali
single dive, all equipment: $50
six dives, all equipment: $300
certified open water course: $420+

MAKUNUDU

Flying......n/a
Speed boat......50 mins
Dhoni......n/a

North Malé Atoll

PITCHED AT THE TOP END OF THE MARKET, MAKUNUDU offers peaceful, relaxing holidays for the well-to-do, in a beautiful, private but still informal environment. In what it sets out to do it succeeds wonderfully.

With the idea of reducing the number of decisions and concerns for the guests, the holidays are **all-inclusive**. That is, full board plus all watersports, a night fishing trip, a snorkel trip and a full day island hop including barbecue. Meals, in the intimate, thoughtfully lit **restaurant**, and prepared by the French chef, are a real pleasure here. An option for breakfast is service in the room or on your balcony. Lunch is an expansive buffet, and dinner is a candlelit delight served at the table. Afternoon tea, as well, is prepared daily.

There are many more staff than possible guests, but they are as discreet as the **service** is good. Flexibility and attention to detail are a hallmark, from the always prompt airport transfer to the wicker cover over the air conditioning units. A

This is undoubtedly a classy resort; it looks good and it feels good

spa and natural beauty centre has recently been opened. The island itself has a long history as a safe anchorage a day's sail from Malé, and something of the mature, cosmopolitan atmosphere has transferred to the present day resort.

Italians and French make up something over half the number of guests, with an

equal mix of Swiss, British, Japanese and Germans filling the other rooms. With just thirty six **rooms** spread among the lush vegetation the sense of calm and privacy is accentuated. Inside the rooms and out, the style is natural and low-key but with no compromises (though they are not particularly big and I found the shower none too strong). The a/c, fully

Relative price:

3

8

Density of rooms to island size:

stocked fridge and safe are nicely 'camouflaged'. Bow windows and a glass door open directly onto the beach.

On the whole the **beach** is very good. Though it is broken up by groynes, these are placed and assessed one by one, and so are not intrusive. The **reef** is also good, its odd shape giving rise to a variety of underwater environments. The watersports and dive centres are efficient, friendly and well stocked.

This is undoubtedly a **classy** resort; it looks good and it feels good. For the well-heeled couple looking to get away from it all on a small equatorial island, this must be on the shortlist.

Resort	tel: 446464	fax: 446565

email: makunudu@dhivehinet.net.mv

can of beer: $3.85	full day-
lime juice: $4.40	island hopping: $45
mineral water: $3.80	sunset fishing: $10

Dive centre   Makunudu
single dive, all equipment: $42
five dives, all equipment: $240
certified open water course: $450

MEEDHUPARU

Flying.....45 mins
Speed boat.....240 mins
Dhoni.....n/a

Raa Atoll

team effort. Every evening there is some sort of organised entertainment, usually in the specially built outdoor theatre, and then it's onto the disco floor until the early hours. Other nationalities are welcome to join in with any of these events.

Organised daytime events utilise some, but by no means all, of the resorts many facilities. Everyday there is group aerobics, canoeing, indoor games competitions, gym work-outs, a volleyball match and dancing sessions. Not forgetting the usual island and fishing excursions. Besides all these, there are tennis courts, beauty salon and, for relaxation, a steam bath, a sauna and an ayurvedic centre. This latter is a rare facility in the Maldives and is not just for relaxation. It is also the serious modern application of ancient healthcare wisdom, based around warm oil and herbal massages. The centre offers a seven day package that works a wonder on your mind and body and may be worth the holiday in itself.

MEEDHUPPARU IS A BRAND NEW RESORT ALONE

in its atoll far to the north of most other resort islands. A little over half the guests here are Italian, with Germans, British and French joining them. But it is the Italians who set the atmosphere for the place.

A significant reason for this is the active presence of Italian animators. They do a great job involving guests in the daily activities and the special events, creating a fun atmosphere of cameraderie. Perhaps less so during the day than other Italian club resorts, but at night it's a full-on

The holiday that most people come for, of course, is based around the beach and the water. And on these matters, Meedhupparu is a mix of the very good and the not so good. The beach is wonderful for three quarters of the island but suffers serious erosion, in the off-season only it must be said, around the south-west section. In the high season (January to April) it should be fine. At the water's edge, the beach slopes down fairly sharply to give an immediate swimming depth but little paddling around width. The lagoon bottom is

Relative price:

7

7

Density of rooms to island size:

smooth and sandy and the reef drop off is always within swimming distance. But the snorkeling is only ok.

The same might also be said of the diving. For some reason there doesn't seem to be quite as much to see as in other atolls. However, this is a brand new resort in a mostly undocumented atoll, dive-wise, so the great sites might not yet have been found.

The two hundred and fifteen rooms are all the same, except for one suite room. Inside, they are fine and have a number of extra facilities, such as hairdryer, safe and tea and coffee maker. There are two wash basins and two showers. Outside, it is all too obvious that they are constructed of raw concrete blocks. Few rooms have a view to the beach, partly because of the thick bush in front and partly because the rooms are tightly fitted in around each other. And yet nearly a quarter of the island, with a beautiful beach, has no rooms at all.

The public areas, particularly the bar and recreation centre have such high ceilings and are so large that there is little chance of them filling up and creating any atmosphere. The large swimming pool, though, is fine. The restaurant may be in the wrong place, but the food served is really a highlight of the resort. The buffets are varied, comprehensive and excellently prepared out of a pristine new kitchen. Successful special events include a lobster night around the pool and a Maldivian night in a rustic setting on the beach.

Meedhupparu was planned and built in near record time and, at the moment, it shows. A year or two down the line, under the guidance of the vastly experienced Sri Lankan operators, it should be altogether much better, when the resort has found its true 'raison d'etre'.

Resort	tel: 230116	fax: 230128
	email: admin@pearlresort.com	
can of beer: $3.50	half day-	
lime juice: $4.00	island hopping: $25	
mineral water: $3.00	sunset fishing: $15	
Dive centre	The Crab	
	single dive, all equipment: $60	
	five dives, all equipment: $330	
	certified open water course: $480	

MEERUFENFUSHI

Flying.....n/a
Speed boat.....60 mins
Dhoni.....n/a

North Malé Atoll

MEERU NOW HAS A SWIMMING POOL. BEFORE IT

was built the repeater guests were, at best, dubious about it. Today it looks as though it has always been there, it's a big hit and it gives the resort a focus it lacked before.

With a large reception building and two huge bars people didn't know where to gather. Now it's everyone round the pool during the day (when not diving or on the beach) and in the next door bar at night (the other bar is used pretty much only for discos).

With the swimming pool, which has a child's pool, Meeru becomes more family oriented and less diver oriented. I should immediately say it's still a great place to go diving from. Almost on its own out on the eastern tip of the atoll, a large number of **dive sites** are not only close by but also not often visited by other resorts. The channels and 'outsides' north of the resort are lonely places where the big pelagics and other rarely sighted fish are happy to swim. Sharks, tuna and barracuda are regularly seen, as well as manta rays during the south-west monsoon and even whale sharks.

The impressive Ocean Pro are the new dive team. Coming in with all new equipment and compressors, they have increased the diving options, such as day trips up to Helengeli, two tank dives and regular night dives. They also run two safari boats which are bookable from reception.

The reef edge is much too far to reach from shore but there is a shuttle boat every hour and a half-day three reef

snorkeling trip every second day. Inside the lagoon there is enough coral and fish to keep novices happy.

The beaches are generally very good. On the west side, looking into the atoll, they are broad and fine even though a few groynes have had to be built to keep them that way. On the east side, looking out to the open ocean, the beach comes and goes, but is usually good. Where the beach diminishes are the remaining

Relative price

10

5

Density of
rooms to
island size:

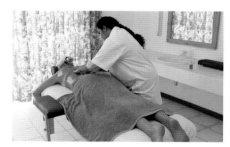

blocks of standard rooms (fifty eight, refurbished and repainted).

Of the two hundred and twenty seven total, a hundred and thirty eight are 'land villas', twenty nine are water bungalows and two are honeymoon suites. That's a lot of rooms even though this is a relatively large island. There are now no secret beaches and a fair amount of land inside the island is now under fruit and vegetable cultivation. Yet it is

still one of the lushest and most fertile resort islands.

The new rooms are entirely of wood and built to a good standard. The two honeymoon suites are something else. Huge, gleaming white and with a large sundeck that looks out uninterrupted to the rising sun. Add a mini hifi, coffee maker, toasted sandwich maker and fridge and it seems they belong to another resort. You can only reach them by boat.

The price for Meeru is still very good. If the place is no longer cheap and cheerful, it's good value and chearful.

Resort	tel: 443157	fax: 445946
	email: meeru@dhivehinet.net.mv	
can of beer: $2		half day-
lime juice: $2		island hopping: $30
mineral water: $2		sunset fishing: $10
Dive centre		Ocean Pro
	single dive, all equipment: $42	
	five dives, all equipment: $200	
	certified open water course: $440	

MIRIHI

Flying......25 mins
Speed boat......120 mins
Dhoni......n/a

Ari Atoll, south-west

〰 **MIRIHI IS A SMALL, NEAT RESORT MUCH LOVED BY THE** Germans and Austrians who come here. It has all the essentials of a good resort including an excellent relationship between the staff and the guests.

Of the forty **rooms** only ten are actually on the island and thirty are water bungalows, all in a row on the north side. Facing north they don't catch the sun on their verandahs and nor, surprisingly, do they have steps down into the lagoon. All the rooms are clean, tidy and well fitted out. They have each been recently renovated. Three of the water bungalows are family size, with room for three beds and a screen.

Being such a **small** island, it is no walk at all over to the other side where the glorious white **beach** stretches all the way down and around the corner, unhindered by any groynes.

Relative price:

8

8

Density of
rooms to
island size:

At the end of the main jetty is a huge bulb of sand, in front of the large and impressive reception. Behind this is the welcoming room and then the comfortable, intimate bar (with one side open to the beach), leading to the dining room. Everything is neat and well organised. Breakfast and lunch are buffet, dinner is set and all the food is more than satisfactory. It is a pleasant change to see a resort serve rice and curry.

The regulars return again and again to enjoy what is almost their own private island.

much better recommendation for a house reef than that. As for the other dive sites, they are mostly some distance away in the well-known channels of southeast Ari Atoll.

However, there are some good, quiet local ones.

Mirihi is not widely known, but the people who come here seem to be happy with that, returning again and again to enjoy what is almost their own private island.

The **dive school** is run by 'Mary & Steve'. Their predecessors, Helmut and Barbara Cornelli published a most attractive underwater book based on the island's own house reef. You can't get a

Resort   tel: 450500   fax: 450501
email: mirihi@dhivehinet.net.mv

can of beer: $3.30	half day-
lime juice: $3.30	island hopping: $25
mineral water: $4.40	sunset fishing: $15

Dive centre   Aqua Base
single dive, all equipment: $61
six dives, all equipment: $336
certified open water course: $425

MOOFUSHI

Flying.....25 mins
Speed boat.....n/a
Dhoni.....n/a

Ari Atoll, west

〰〰 NEARLY EVERYBODY ON
MOOFUSHI IS ITALIAN, AND
compared to other Italian resorts it is
probably more easy-going and less
expensive. Sadly, it doesn't have much
else going for it.

The main problem is erosion. In
attempts to control it, **walls** have been
built up against the rooms and inside the
lagoon. But matters have only got worse
and more of the remaining beach has
been eroded. Some rooms have hindered

access to the water. And where there is beach outside the rooms, there is a wall a metre or two into the water.

The **rooms** themselves are tasteful and unusually large. Each room has a telephone and minibar. The fittings in the bathroom are not of a high standard. Of the sixty rooms fifteen are water bungalows and these are very well placed in a row parallel to the island's best **reef**. The south facing verandahs have steps down to the water and a short swim takes you to the reef edge.

There is some excellent **diving** close by, with channels both sides of the island full of the big pelagics and caves replete with large schools of reef fish. Currents can be strong so they are not for beginners, though a number of dives inside the atoll are suitable.

The reception, bar and restaurant **buildings** are tall and thatched. They are attractive looking from the outside and, in the evening under low lights, comfortable and relaxing. But the original building materials used were not of a high standard and the Italian company now running the resort is slowly replacing everything to bring the standard up.

Finally, for an Italian resort the **food** is just not what you would expect.

Occupancy on Moofushi is remarkably high, so many people do enjoy it here. If you don't demand a perfect beach, and you get a very good price for your holiday, I dare say you'll have a great time.

Relative price:

6

9

Density of rooms to island size:

Resort   *tel*: 450517   *fax*: 450509
  email: moofushi@dhivehinet.net.mv

can of beer: $3.00	half day-
lime juice: $2.50	island hopping: $n/a
mineral water: $3.00	sunset fishing: $10

Dive centre   Moofushi
  single dive, all equipment: $55
  five dives, all equipment: $275
  certified open water course: $380

NAKATCHAFUSHI

Flying....n/a
Speed boat....45 mins
Dhoni....105 mins

North Malé Atoll

〰 **THIS IS AN EXCEPTIONALLY POPULAR RESORT, AND IT IS** not hard to see why. The environment is beautiful, the atmosphere is informal yet the service is top notch.

Fifty one **rooms** are almost hidden in a green canopy of coconut palms above and a very carefully tended **garden** of imported flowers and shrubs below. The effect is not entirely natural Maldivian, but no one's complaining. The rooms themselves, though close and numerous, are of average size, neat, tidy and well fitted out (a/c, minibar, piped music). The bathrooms are very good, with quality fittings.

Piped music follows you to the bar and restaurants. The main **bar** is large, comfy and, in the evening, bubbling with noise and activity. Nearly everyone is on half board, having lunch in the **coffee shop**, either inside, or under the palms between the pool and the sandy lagoon. The food in the main **restaurant** is OK, if rather ordinary. There is also a speciality Asian restaurant.

The **reef** edge is near for two thirds of the circumference and far away for the other one third. This gives people plenty of space for swimming and watersports, but also allows easy access to the drop off for snorkeling. The corals are now back in good condition, after some trouble with the crown-of-thorns starfish.

There is no questioning that level of attachment to a place.

Fish continue to be abundant. Diving is well-organised and quality, fast new boats are used.

The **beaches** are very good indeed. There are some intermittent and fairly prominent groynes. That is a price one often pays for long stretches fine sand.

Nakatcha is much loved by its clientèle. Nearly all the guests are either German or English, and it is said that eighty five percent, in any given week, are 'returnees'. Many of them fax directly to the resort to reserve specific rooms. There's no questioning that level of attachment to a place.

Resort   *tel*: 443847   *fax*: 442665
email:nakatcha@dhivehinet.net.mv

can of beer: $3.30   half day-
lime juice: $6.60   island hopping: $45
mineral water: $3.30   sunset fishing: $14

Dive centre   Nakatcha
single dive, all equipment: $40
six dives, all equipment: $210
certified open water course: $500

NIKA

⌇⌇ NIKA IS THE DIVEHI NAME OF A CERTAIN SHELL

and of the banyan tree. The shell is their emblem and the resort is named after the tree. An enormous banyan tree grows in the middle of the island, clearing the rest of the canopy and plainly visible from out at sea.

As a resort it is probably the most **private** of all. The simple reason for this is that there is only one path around the island and it is inside, behind the bungalows. With careful growth of bushes and trees one is unable to see the neighbouring bungalows and it's quite difficult to even visit them. There is an unspoken rule here that you do not cross this privacy boundary. This means no jogging on the beach.

Each bungalow has its own private **beach** front. The price to pay for this is the sight of groynes. Almost every bungalow has two groynes either side of its plot. Some of these are low and unobtrusive walls, but others are large and frequent. On the other hand they are the best constructed and maintained groynes in the country.

The beaches themselves are good to very good. And the **lagoon** is excellent, not too large or too shallow. The coral starts at a good distance away and the reef edge is never far, so it is good for both swimming and snorkeling. One surprise, on this classy resort, is the beach furniture: white plastic chairs and white plastic loungers (though these have a cotton mattress cover).

Relative price:

3

2

Density of rooms to island size:

The **rooms** were designed, like the whole island, by an Italian architect. They are undoubtedly in the top few of all the resort rooms (I would put Sonevafushi's, Kuda Huraa's and Banyan Tree's up with them). It is not one round design but several curving spaces coming off each other, like the inside of a shell.

Nika has been one of the very best for many years now

The sitting room, bedroom and shower/washroom are all large. The shower/washroom itself is bigger than many resorts' bedroom and shower room together. There is no a/c (anywhere on the island) and it is completely unmissed with the abundant slatted windows, high roof and quiet ceiling fan.

There is no reception, but one enters from the main jetty into a lovely, curvy and comfortable **lounge** and bar. At the end of the other jetty is the restaurant, and whenever the weather is fine **dining** is outside on the deck. Dining is, as expected, of the first class. Only the finest ingredients are imported. Breakfast

and lunch are buffet, five of the evening meals are set, and two are barbecues on the beach. At any time, however, you may order in advance some dish you would particularly like and it will be prepared for you at no extra cost.

That is really part of the philosophy of the place. It is very expensive but once here you will not be surprised by a big bill for extras. For example, the telephone and fax charges are possibly the

cheapest of any resort. Windsurfing and canoes are free and so are sunset fishing, tennis, badminton and bowls.

Morning trawler **fishing** is also offered, and one unique fishing experience - shark fishing, where you set off in the afternoon, sleep on the fishing dhoni and return the next morning. Nika is fortunate to share an uninhabited island for other full and half-day excursions.

This used to be an all-Italian resort but now it is about two thirds Italian, with Germans around ten percent, French at five percent and a few Japanese. It is a private but decidedly friendly kind of place.

Nika has been around a long time, and on top of the tree for most of that time. It has hit upon a great formula and its maintenance is excellent, so I expect it will stay in the very top bracket for a good many years more.

Resort	*tel*: 450516	*fax*: 450577
	email: nika@dhivehinet.net.mv	
can of beer: $4		half day-
lime juice: $4		island hopping: $16
mineral water: $3		sunset fishing: $incl.
Dive centre		R & R
	single dive, all equipment: $75	
	Ten dives, all equipment: $299	
	certified open water course: $499	

PALM BEACH

Flying.....35 mins
Speed boat.....n/a
Dhoni.....n/a

Lhaviyani Atoll

ON AN OLD, ONCE IN-HABITED ISLAND, PALM
Beach successfully maintains the line between minimal impact and full facilities.

There are no groynes or sea walls here, the beaches are allowed to shift with the seasons. In the long run this is the best idea, but it does mean that, seasonally, some rooms have very little beach outside. This is particularly the case with the twenty, more expensive, two-storied, Villa rooms. On the other hand, these rooms are built in the shady, palm and flower studded end of the island, near to the main buildings and the delightful, specialist restaurant.

The opposite half of the island is more or less open to the skies and here we find the Superior (25) and Deluxe (45) rooms. The advantage of these rooms is as one moves further away from the public area everything becomes even more quiet and the beaches even more untouched. The rooms themselves are large and pleasant enough, though, like all the buildings here, rather too 'blocky'. Plans to introduce specially designed textiles, patterned on the traditional mat designs, will bring a welcome warmth.

All the rooms have piped music, televi-

Relative price:

5

5

Density of
rooms to
island size:

sions with many satellite channels and in-house movies. It is in the nature of this place that everything is laid on but nothing is pushed. All watersports, apart from diving, are free for the asking. As is tennis, squash, table tennis and pool. All excursions and fishing trips are also free. The guest relations people and the tour reps quietly move through the restaurant in the evenings chatting and informing guests about what is happening at any time.

It is an unfortunate fact that after constructing all the main buildings to deal with 180 rooms, 100 only were built, so the main bar, coffee shop and restaurant are too big for the number of guests at any one time. The intimate atmosphere engendered by drinks and live music in the pool bar is disappears into the open spaces of the vaste restaurant.

The food, though, is faultless. An Italian bias to a continental cuisine, it is all

fresh, varied and sure to satisfy. The salads and deserts are unusually good, as is the sizzling meat and fish grill outside. Although almost everyone is on full board, there is a temptation at some point to check out the small, classy a la carte restaurant, beautifully sited beside the beach, beneath the palms.

Italians are a little over half the population here and the ambience is molded by them, but now there are many Swiss, French and Japanese also enjoying what the resort offers. Essentially what it offers is good food, large rooms, lots of facilities and a varied, pretty island.

Resort	tel: 230084	fax: 230084
	email: palmbech@dhivehinet.net.mv	

can of beer: $4.00	half day-
lime juice: $4.00	island hopping: incl.
mineral water: $3.00	sunset fishing: incl.

Dive centre   Macana
single dive, all equipment: $52
five dives, all equipment: $260
certified open water course: $425+

PARADISE ISLAND

Flying.....n/a
Speed boat.....20 mins
Dhoni.....n/a

North Malé Atoll

〰 PEOPLE EITHER LOVE PARADISE ISLAND OR THEY

know they have made a mistake as soon as they step off the jetty. This is not a small, cosy resort. It is large, modern and active. No resort has more *facilities* and few match its level of *service*.

Not only are the staff noticeably well trained, at every level, but each one, it seems, is friendly and helpful. As this resort is close to Malé and the inter-national airport it is also aimed at the business community and visiting VIPs, so the service and facilities reflect this.

The conference centre is unlikely to be used by holidaymakers, but then there is the gym, sauna, squash court, badminton court, tennis courts, volleyball court, table tennis and snooker tables. (The squash and badminton courts do not have air conditioning and so are extremely hot to play in). On top of this there is the fullest range of watersports facilities: catamaran, windsurf and canoe, parasail, water-ski and jet-ski.

Diving is, of course, available and there are a large number of excellent sites very close by, including a Manta Point.

As for evening *entertainments* there is always something going on, from fire limbo and crab racing to disco and live bands. And a special karaoke lounge too. No one complains of having nothing to do here! On the other hand, it is possible

Each room has everything you could ask for: from bidet and hairdryer to a ten channel satellite t.v.

Relative price:

6

8

Density of rooms to island size:

to spend the day on the beach and get away from everyone in the evening by eating and drinking in one of the alternative restaurants and bars.

As well as the main **restaurant**, which is very good, there is a Japanese restaurant, and two restaurant/bars at the very end of the jetty and the water bungalow walkway. One, facing the sunset, is an Italian restaurant, the other, facing the sunrise, is for seafood.

There are forty water bungalows and two hundred and sixty **rooms** in all - the third largest resort in the country. There is little difference between the rooms, except for the views of, and steps down into, the lagoon. Each room has everything you could ask for and probably more: from a bidet and hairdryer to a

large ten channel satellite t.v. and fully-stocked minibar. What the room doesn't have is any character or personal touch, but the bed is comfortable and everything else is clean, tidy and bright.

Not all the rooms are well situated, however. This is a very new island, in that much of it is reclaimed from the lagoon and some rooms are in areas that are not yet fully developed in terms of flowers, trees and, crucially, beaches. On the whole the **beaches** are remarkably good for being reclaimed, and the head gardener has done a marvellous job.

The **lagoon** is huge, shallow and, for the most part, without coral, so swimming is OK, but snorkeling is a disappointment. For this reason snorkelling trips are organised, but you must pay for them.

Indeed, it is sometimes a complaint here that any and every 'extra' is charged for. On the other hand, the price of beer and mineral water has come down.

Still, most people who come here have a great holiday. In terms of facilities, activities and service this resort is second to none. If you want options and choices, in a modern but easy-going environment, then this is it.

Resort	tel: 440011	fax: 440022
	email: paradise@dhivehinet.net.mv	
can of beer: $3.00		half day-
lime juice: $2.75		island hopping: $25
mineral water: $2.75		sunset fishing: $20
Dive centre		Delphis
		single dive, all equipment: $60
		five dives, all equipment: $300
		certified open water course: $560

RANVELI

Flying......25 mins
Speed boat......n/a
Dhoni......n/a

Ari Atoll, south-east

RANVELI IS UNUSUAL IN SEVERAL WAYS, IN THE GEO-graphy of the island and the design of the buildings. What is not unusual is to find a large number of Italians having a great time. This is another one hundred percent, full board, **Club Vacanza** resort.

The sand on this **thin** channel island has been pushed down to one end, creating a marvellous wide **beach** that winds away into the lagoon. For sunbathing, volley-ball and generally 'getting together' this is the perfect spot. In fact, it is just about the only one outside, as the rest of the island has a very narrow beach, if any at all. The other place to hang out is the small but decent swimming pool.

All around the sandy beach and the south side of the island, the **lagoon** is extensive and very shallow - good for sitting and wading around in (but no good for watersports). The lagoon on the other side is almost non-existent. The **reef** edge drop-off is only ten or fifteen metres from shore. This means great snorkeling is within easy reach. Though

not many rooms have a good beach outside their door, it is only a few steps to the big beach or to the snorkelling.

Perhaps the nearby reef excites people, but there are probably more **divers** here than on any other Italian resort. Anything up to forty guests head out twice a day, in three or four boats, to dive the excellent local sites. This south-east corner has some of the best diving in the atoll, indeed, some of the best of any of the resort atolls.

Other day-time **excursions** in a full programme include sunset fishing, trawler fishing, visiting uninhabited islands and resort island hopping. Night snorkelling and snorkelling trips are also organised. Unlike most other Club Vacanza resorts nothing is included in the price here, you must even pay to hire your snorkel. Guests know this and it doesn't seem to dampen their spirits.

In a small **cabaret** theatre there are nightly amateur shows and comedy evenings. And after every meal, it seems, there are dancing sessions. These take

Relative price

6

10

Density of rooms to island size:

place in the unique nineteenth century style **pier** that stretches out over the water. Cool and light, with open sides, it also manages to be intimate, with its many decorations of painted glass, leaded chandeliers

and arched fan lights evoking a bygone time of leisure and ease. A fine place for eating and drinking.

Breakfast and lunch are buffet, dinner is set - but with a buffet vegetable and salad selection. The **food** is, as always, very good indeed. Each of the Club Vacanza resorts boasts that even with two styles of pasta a day you can have a two week holiday and never repeat a dish. Afternoon tea is also served daily.

Perhaps the only complaint heard here is that, for such a small island, there are too many rooms. There are fifty six in all and they are in two-storey blocks of four, taking up most of the island. For many people this isn't a problem, as just about everything happens around the outside of the island and during the day many people leave on excursions. But to some

people it migh well be a deterrent.

The **rooms** themselves are a good size, pleasantly decorated and with individual balconies. The coir flooring is unique and both appropriate and attractive. The facilities are all that you would expect. There is a/c, plenty of hot and cold water, a telephone and a full minibar.

Resort	tel: 450570	fax: 450523
	email:	
can of beer: $?		half day-
lime juice: $?		island hopping: $?
mineral water: $?		sunset fishing: $?
Dive centre		Ranveli
	single dive, all equipment: $?	
	five dives, all equipment: $?	
	certified open water course: $?	

REETHI BEACH

Flying.....35 mins
Speed boat.....n/a
Dhoni.....n/a

Baa Atoll

THE ISLAND HAS TERRIFIC NATURAL ASSETS, the resort has excellent facilities, only the quality of the buildings makes it less than a top ranking resort.

The beach is wide, warm white and fine. It narrows down the flanks of the island but is still good. Strangely, the path doesn't go all the way around but moves inland, making a third of the beach inaccessible unless you walk around the outside. But, on the other hand, where there are rooms there's a good beach and that's the important bit.

The lagoon is ideal. On both sides the drop off is nearby but what makes this even better is the fact that one side is a classic reef edge (best for snorkelling) while the other side drops to a large, deep lagoon. This latter is perfect for swimming and watersports, being deep but also protected from waves and strong currents. And the watersports centre is fully stocked, enthusiastically run and well used. Fully stocked means jet skis, waterskiing, parasailing and peddle boats as well as the usual catamarans and windsurfers. To top it off there are a couple of nearby sandbanks and uninhabited islands to aim for.

There are two outdoor tennis courts and, in a non a/c but fairly well ventilated building, two squash courts, badminton courts and table tennis tables. And a well equipped a/c gym.

What more? Well the food is excellent. There's a specialist Chinese restaurant and a Grill that's used for the results of the sunset fishing and special occasions.

But the main restaurant food is pretty special anyway – stuffed cuttlefish in lobster sauce, chicken roulade, varied salads with balsamic vinegar...

The problem is, the built surrounding is just not up to the content. This resort was maybe the very first of the new batch of resorts to open, back in November 1998, and it shows. The buildings are 'blocks', all made of concrete fronted with varnished plywood boards. Almost everything speaks of the speed of construction. A new management took over in 2000 and time and

Relative price

8

7

Density of rooms to island size:

decoration will improve things.

Guests on all-inclusive packages have a separate bar to have their snacks and drink in. This can be seen as a private 'club' or it can be seen as depriving them of mixing socially in the evening with everyone else.

Of the one hundred rooms, forty are superior, thirty deluxe and thirty waterbungalows. The superiors are in lines whereas the deluxes are separate, though close, and have 'swing joli' in front. The base of the rooms on the outside are attractively designed like the base of historic coral stone mosques. The waterbungalows have infrared internet access through the television, but don't

have steps down to the water. All the rooms are furnished in a comfortable but fairly basic manner.

Until this resort was opened there was only one resort in the atoll (Sonevafushi) so the diving here is to sites that are rarely visited. Reethi Beach commands a major channel in the north-east of the atoll and so has a great variety of nearby sites to choose from. The fish life is exceptional, particularly the ocean-going pelagics that use the channel as a short cut. Apparently a whale shark hung around for ten days in November '99. With up to four dives a day and a night dive every other day, if diving is your priority you'll be happy here, no doubt.

Resort   tel: 232626   fax: 232727
email: info@reethibeach.com.mv

can of beer: $3.50   half day-
lime juice: $4.50   island hopping: $47
mineral water: $3.50   sunset fishing: $20

Dive centre   Sea Explorer
single dive, all equipment: $?
five dives, all equipment: $?
certified open water course: $?

REETHI RAH

Flying.....n/a
Speed boat.....45 mins
Dhoni.....150 mins

North Malé Atoll

REETHI RAH IS AN OLD RESORT WITH A 'LOCAL ISLAND' feel. There is a charm to the natural appearance and easy-going management, but there is also an edge of inattention and disrepair. Still, the beach and the windsurfing are undeniably good.

On this long, thin island that runs due north/south, the **beach** facing into the atoll is wonderful: cream coloured, fine and completely uninterrupted by groyne or wall. Occasionally the thick vegetation reaches down close to the water, but this only creates smaller, private stretches of beach. The lagoon floor, too, is all soft sand.

The other side of the island is another story. A line of pitted coral rock runs the whole length of the island. It is not attractive but it protects the very narrow beach from the battering currents of the open sea. There is room enough to draw up a deck chair and enjoy a quiet time. The only things visible on this side are the coffee shop on stilts and the water bungalows at the north end.

The **lagoon** around the whole island is very large and sandy bottomed. This makes it ideal for swimming and watersports. **Windsurfing**, for beginners in particular, is understandably popular. On the other hand, the snorkeling is

pretty hopeless. Even if you reach the reef edge it is still recovering from an old crown-of-thorns starfish infestation. **Diving** in the region, however, is still excellent, with many renowned sites in the large channel to the north, especially the Protected Marine Area of Makunudhoo Kandu.

Opened way back in 1979, the resort still looks more like a local island than a purpose-built resort. There are actually few coconut palms but the vegetation is dense overhead and the atmosphere is cool and shady. The fallen leaves are swept into the undergrowth and a lily-lined path leads you through.

The fallen leaves are swept into the undergrowth and a lily-lined path leads you through.

Relative price:

5

4

Density of rooms to island size:

Benign neglect works well with nature but not so well with man-made structures. The bar and restaurant, at least, could do with redecoration and the rooms could do with a refit. It is unpretentious and you don't pay top money for a holiday here, but still, so many other resorts are getting smarter all the time.

Of the sixty **rooms** in total, ten are water bungalows. These are a bit more expensive and don't have good snorkeling, but they are near a beach and they are larger, brighter and newer than the beach bungalows. The latter are solidly built and separate, but the fixtures and fittings inside are really showing their age. Although a fridge and telephone have been put in, there is no a/c or hot water and the overall decoration is not what you might expect. Furthermore, the management are none too concerned.

Looking on the bright side, you don't spend long in your room. The really important things are good: the water is crystal clear and the beach is terrific.

Resort	*tel*: 441905	*fax*: 441906
	email: rrresort@dhivehinet.net.mv	

can of beer: $3.30	half day-
lime juice: $2.75	island hopping: $17
mineral water: $3.85	sunset fishing: $16

Dive centre   Eurodivers
single dive, all equipment: $42
six dives, all equipment: $252
certified open water course: $476

RIHIVELI

Flying.....n/a
Speed boat.....50 mins
Dhoni.....n/a

South Malé Atoll

That is not to say it is snobby. It is run by a lively and sympathetic group of mostly young people who do their best to make sure everybody feels at home. It is the kind of place where you can retreat to quietly enjoy the luxury, or you can fill each day with activity and each evening with sociability.

Of course, most people mix it, and for this Rihiveli is excellent. At any time, free of charge, guests can pick up a windsurfer, canoe or catamaran, and even go water-skiing. Each day there are two free trips to one of fifteen local snorkeling

The secret of the island's charms is jealously kept by the discerning couples who come here

sites. In the evening, table tennis competitions, and the like, are regular events. Parasailing, game fishing and a variety of excursions are also organised. All excursions are free.

This is an **all-inclusive** resort in the best sense. It is the only resort in the country that has fresh, chilled water freely available not only in the rooms but also the restaurant. And as to the restaurant (built over the water), the full-board arrangement includes a good choice of buffets and barbecues as well as an à la carte menu. You don't even have to turn up at the restaurant for lunch, you can wade out or canoe to the neighbouring desert island and there, every day at one o'clock, a barbecue lunch is served.

RIHIVELI IS A GORGEOUS RESORT WITH A DISTINCTIVE

French look and a cultured ambience. Alone on the southern tip of South Malé Atoll, the secret of the island's charms, it seems, is jealously kept by the discerning couples who have discovered it, and return year after year after year.

In fact there is not one but two small, uninhabited islands within Rihiveli's vast lagoon. Shallow and sandy, it is not a perfect lagoon, but a platform is moored in the deeper water for water-skiing, a 'swimming pool' has been dredged nearby and the snorkeling trips make up for the lack of a reef.

Protected by this lagoon (and a few groynes), the **beaches** are excellent around the whole island. Set back and shaded by sculptured bushes, but still in view of the sand and water, are the forty eight rooms, two to a 'cottage'.

Simplicity and **elegance** are the key words here, obvious from the moment you first walk along the jetty: sandy, irregular but solid, with grasses sprouting along the edge like a French country lane. The resort's central focus is the beautifully designed bar/lounge and games room building. With echoes of the South Pacific, the high thatched roofs slope sharply and reach low to the ground around the open sides. Inside it is cool, shady and comfortable.

The South Pacific flavour is taken further (perhaps a tad too far for some tastes) with the blowing of a conch shell to announce meals, and a tame parrot at the bar who sings the first phrase of the Marseillaise. A distinctly Western touch is the playing of classical music onto the beach outside the bar at sunset every day, as guests gather to enjoy a sundowner.

No doubt about it, if you like the sound of this place, you'll love a holiday here.

Resort	*tel*: 443731	*fax*: 440052
	email: info@rihiveliisland.com	
can of beer: $2.80	half day-	
lime juice: $2.00	island hopping: $inc.	
mineral water: $3.00	sunset fishing: $inc.	
Dive centre	Eurodivers	
	single dive, all equipment: $43	
	five dives, all equipment: $205	
	certified open water course: $471	

SONEVAFUSHI

Flying.....30 mins
Speed boat.....n/a
Dhoni.....n/a

Baa Atoll

comparison, the next largest, Kuredu, has three hundred). And what an island. Few, if any, other islands equal the growth and variety of vegetation. Probably most native palms, trees and bushes are here. It is a pleasure and an education to explore along the sandy paths that cut through the jungle canopy. Bicycles are provided to do just that.

Varying in size and luxury, the rooms are divided into six categories, from the small but perfectly formed Rehendi rooms to the lavish extravagance of the Presidential suite. Throughout, natural materials are used exclusively. Much is made of local coconut wood, bamboo and thatch and many objects are crafted from unadorned 'finds'. It's as if Robinson Crusoe had decided not to return to civilization, but to open a resort instead.

Carved out of their own pocket of jungle each room is a few metres away from a beach that runs right around the island, untainted by a single groyne or wall. The reef drop off is never more than a short swim away.

ꙅ SONEVAFUSHI IS STILL THE FINEST RESORT IN THE MALDIVES.

Indeed, it has a growing reputation as one of the finest resorts in South and South-east Asia. It is that good. Inevitably it is as expensive as you would expect such a place to be. But if you really wish to experience the best of Maldivian nature combined with excellence in design and hospitality, then this is the place.

Just sixty two rooms are built on this the largest resort island in the country. (For

It's unfair how good this island is. Just a patch of it is used to grow most of the herbs and salad greens required and many of the vegetables. Put to excellent use by the multinational chefs, the dining on the resort is second to none. One

Relative price:

1

Density of rooms to island size:

of the two restaurants serves predominantly European, particularly Southern European, dishes and the other a fusion of Eastern and Western tastes, with some entirely Eastern dishes. A semellier will help you choose between the three hundred listed wines, that range from thirty-five to five hundred dollars a bottle.

There are a few resorts in the same league but none of them are better

The two restaurants are on opposite sides of the island, one beside the main bar, the other on the beach near the new library, Barefoot shop and small conference room. A glorious spa is tucked away inland. Even when the island is full, guests hardly run into each other and are surprised to meet so many others at the weekly cocktail party given by the general manager on a nearby sandbank.

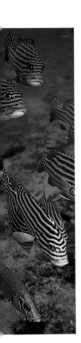

There are no evening entertainments and daytime excursions are in the line of champagne breakfasts on lonely sandbanks and sunset cruises for two. If you want to book such a trip or sort out just about anything else, you give a ring to your designated guest relations officer; the reception hardly exists as such.

Everything about this place exudes class. If you can afford it, this is the best there is.

Resort	*tel*: 230304	*fax*: 230374
	email: sonresa@soneva.com.mv	
can of beer: $4.40		full day-
lime juice: $3.85		island hopping: $100
mineral water: $3.85		sunset fishing: $30
Dive centre		Soleni
	single dive, all equipment: $80	
	five dives, all equipment: $190	
	certified open water course: $360	

SUMMER ISLAND

∾∾ WHAT WAS ONCE A ROUGH AND READY DIVE ISLAND HAS been transformed into a middle market, mellow all-inclusive resort. It is not the most beautiful of islands, but that is soon unnoticed, thanks to the special efforts of the long-term manager and amicable staff.

Meals are three buffets a day plus tea and sandwiches at four o'clock. Each evening meal is themed: Mongolian, Italian, Carvery, International, Barbecue and Oriental. And occasionally prawn or lobster evenings are set up on the beach for a $30 supplement. All regular drinks are free, only premium spirits and wines must be paid for. Both the restaurant and bar are cool, dim thatched places with sandy floors.

In addition to food and drink, one island hopping, one night fishing and two snorkel trips a day are included. The house reef is not really accessible from the beach so up to six speedboat trips a day are made to nearby snorkelling spots. The large lagoon is perfect, however, for watersports and that centre is well-placed and stocked with just about everything.

The dive base leaders, Lydia and Michael, have lived here for eighteen years so far. Of course by now they know every hidden tila and cave in the neighbourhood. They run an efficient centre and know all their divers by name and proficiency. With forty odd sites within an hour's dhoni ride, diving is very good here and, or but (depending how you look at it), the change to all-inclusive has significantly reduced the number of regular divers.

The ninety two standard rooms are pretty tightly spaced around the three sides of the island and include a two storey block of twelve rooms (some people ask especially for the upstairs rooms). The base of the triangle has the best beach

Relative price:

9

10

Density of
rooms to
island size:

*The dive centre
provides an almost individual
service.*

and uninterupted views. One long side has a low wall just in front of the beach, while the third side has a wall set in the lagoon. The rooms are of a good standard, simple, neat and all with a/c and a third bed, but no 'extras'.

At the tip of the island are sixteen new waterbungalows in four blocks of four. These are large, solid and square, similar to the Embudu Village ones, even down to the plate glass in the wooden floors. All the extra facilities are here, minibar, phone, hairdryer and satellite tv, with

two sports channels. It is a handsome room with good views out to the reef and the horizon. But on deck you are entirely visible to your three near neighbours.

The third bed in each room encourages families to come and other details encourage return visits. The dive base gives a discount if you go back and you will find fruit and wine in your room upon arrival. Then there is the cake for every birthday and anniversary and the fruit and beach dining or T shirt if you are on honeymoon. With a successful gardening

effort that has beautified the inside of the island, these things reflect a thoughtful management.

German speakers make up around eighty percent of guests here with British making up the rest.

Resort	tel: 443088 fax: 441910
	email: siv@dhivehinet.net.mv

can of beer: $incl.	half day-
lime juice: $incl.	island hopping: $1 incl.
mineral water: $incl.	sunset fishing: $1 incl.

Dive centre	Diving
	single dive, all equipment: $46
	six dives, all equipment: $276
	certified open water course: $490

SUN ISLAND

Flying.....35 mins
Speed boat.....150 mins
Dhoni.....n/a

Ari Atoll, south

〰 SUN ISLAND IS TO MALDIVES WHAT TEXAS IS TO THE UNITED States. Everything here is on the grand scale. This is the largest resort in the country with the most facilities, the biggest pool and the largest buffets. Here too is that odd mix of brash modernity and rich old world decoration. Finally, it shares the same generous and genuine feel for service.

The level of service, the number of facilities, the overall build quality and the expense of the furnishings take this resort into the five star category. But you don't get a five star bill for staying here, so the value for money is, at the moment, excellent.

No other resort in the country has a putting green. And, typically of the owner, no expense has been spared to make this one perfect. The special grass seeds were imported from the USA, underneath is a complex sand filtration system, consultants have spent months on this one job, and so on.

Running beside the green is a broad, paved boulevard lined with tall palms. On the other side are pristine tennis, volley and basketball courts. It is like something out of Meditteranean Spain or California. It is not 'typically Maldivian', but then things have been moving away from the typically Maldivian for years now, as the expectation of luxury as well as nature steadily increases.

Having said that, Sun Island received the first Presidential Green Award, indicating that great efforts have been made behind the scenes to ensure the resort is ecologically friendly. And the island's rich soil supports many majestic coconut palms. Birdsong is heard at dawn and dusk, which is not common. The beaches

are superb all the way around, without groynes. The large, soft-bottomed lagoon is ideal for swimming and watersports.

The dive centre is run by a pro-active young Dutchman who, typically of the place, tries never to say 'no'. There is almost nothing that cannot be done to accommodate the wishes of the guests. The diving is some of the best in the atoll. Channels, corners and outside reefs are the mainstay, offering chances to see the big pelagics, from rainbow runners to

Relative price:

6

6

Density of
rooms to
island size:

whale sharks. Discovery dives for the inexperienced are also popular here.

*The biggest of
them all,
with the most
of everything*

Snorkeling is not the best around. It is only really feasible off the end of the jetty, which faces into the atoll. There is no drop-off but a gentle slope. Still, the fish are numerous and the excellent Italian/Japanese restaurant at this point along the jetty acts as a daytime rendez-vous and coffee shop.

On the opposite side of the island are the water bungalows. These are the most

expensive rooms (apart from the two 'presidential suite' water bungalows) and the service for these rooms is particularly high (butler service and separate dining). On the land, there is little to differenti-ate between the deluxe and super deluxe rooms, apart from an inside shower and bath. All the rooms share the same solid build and heavy, rich furnishings.

Although Sun Island is obviously a very large resort with every tick box checked (from sauna and massage to jet ski and wake boarding, to say nothing of the packed video games room), it is a collection of small things that truly show the intentions of a hotel. Here, all the chairs and sun loungers are wooden not white plastic, the pool bar offers fresh fruit and juices, and all the coffee throughout is not Nescafe but freshly

ground beans. The grand style of Sun Island is not to everybody's taste but the attention to detail and the service will never disappoint.

Resort	*tel:* 443088	*fax:* 441910
	email:	
	can of beer: $incl.	half day-
	lime juice: $incl.	island hopping: $1 incl.
	mineral water: $incl.	sunset fishing: $1 incl.
Dive centre		Diving
	single dive, all equipment: $46	
	six dives, all equipment: $276	
	certified open water course: $490	

TAJ CORAL REEF

Flying.....n/a
Speed boat.....45 mins
Dhoni.....n/a

North Malé Atoll

THIS SMALL, NEAT AND PRETTY RESORT IS RUN BY the Taj group, India's leading luxury hotel company. The top-class, commited management continues to evolve a first rate product on a carefully cultured island. But the force of nature has caused a few problems around the edges.

Compared to most resorts an extra effort has been put into recreation. Apart from all the usual outings (including Male'), a glass-bottomed boat is available and the diving dhoni is borrowed for champagne cruises (choose from moonlight, starlight and sunset). Stingray feeding is a daily event, photoflights are promoted and there's even a horticultural tour by the Indian gardener. The full evening entertainment list includes unusual options such as acrobats, bingo and bodu beru (cultural show) on the beach with both men and women. And while we're at it, the island has a fitness centre, jacuzzi, swimmingpool, table tennis and snooker table and a wonderful spa out of Bali.

All these things are not pushed but merely there for the asking. In the same way there's an extra variety in the meals and the way you can take them. The main restaurant provides three buffet meals a day, with differently themed every day of the week (Maldivian, Italian, Barbecue, Mexican, Chinese and Seafood). On the beach a small a la carte restaurant specialises in curries and grills. Then there are the special lobster and prawn candlelit nights on the beach. The quality is very good, but I was surprised that there was no variety in the coffee, just Nescafe.

The sixty five room total is made up of thirty five garden villas and thirty lagoon villas. These rooms are essentially the same but the lagoon villas are a little longer and their fittings and textiles are of an even better quality. Both types of

rooms enjoy a unified interior decor of light earth colours. The tea and coffee making facility is a thoughtful addition while the satellite tv, minibar and safe are now almost standard at this level. The view from the lagoon villas is wonderful if your eye doesn't rest on the netted coral walls that arc around this section of the island, made necessary by the oncoming channel current.

Service and commitment from the top Indian hotel group

The housereef diving and snorkeling happens on the leeward side of the island. The reef slopes in stages; first to five metres, then twelve then twenty. At twenty there is a wreck with schools of fish and a large resident napolean wrasse. Diving is popular here, particularly with the Japanese.

Each garden villa is near to the beach, which is wide and fine at low tide but at high tide erosion is evidenced by the low wall built at the shoreline and the visible palmtree roots. At this time you can move onto the permanent bulge of beach on the southeast corner or take time out to snooze in your personal hammock.

It is clear that great effort and care has been put into creating a resort which looks great, has first class facilities and a beautiful landscape. If those are your priorities this must be on your shortlist.

Relative price:

5

8

Density of rooms to island size:

Resort	tel: 441948 fax: 443884
	email: tajcr@dhivehinet.net.mv

can of beer: $4	half day-
lime juice: $3	island hopping: $1 incl.
mineral water: $3	sunset fishing: $1 incl.

Dive centre   Blue in
single dive, all equipment: $58
six dives, all equipment: $270
certified open water course: $500

TARI VILLAGE

Flying.....n/a
Speed boat.....30 mins
Dhoni.....90 mins

North Malé Atoll

〜〜 **TARI VILLAGE HAS MADE A SMART MOVE. IT HAS ADDED** the word Sporting to its name and concentrated on just that.

As a palm-fringed, dream-beach resort it is second to just about every other in the country; as a diving and surfing resort it is second to none. Add to this the easy cameraderie of like-minded people and you have the recipe for a great holiday.

There are just two tour operators. Atoll Travel (run by local legend Tony Hinde) brings in all the surfers and Sun Travel of Male' brings in everybody else. The guests are an odd but amicable mix of Australians, Italians and Japanese. The average age is higher and families are most welcome.

The surf is at its best during the south-west monsoon (the low season). Owing to

Relative price:

10

6

Density of
rooms to
island size:

the shape of the reefs there are a number local waves that are frequent and perfectly formed. Pasta Point is said to be world class, and is just twenty metres away from the CoBar.

The diving too is excellent in the region. The Protected Marine Area of HP Reef, a couple of minutes away, is a highlight among thirty nearby sites. The 'outside' and channel mouth dives offer chances to sight the rare whale shark.

The small island has just twenty four, surprisingly large and well decorated, rooms. Upstairs is a king-size bed, with a single bed on the ground floor. Each room has hot water in the shower, a (weakish) a/c, a telephone and a fridge.

Re-established as family-friendly diving and surfing centre

The island itself is frankly unattractive, with messy walls, vegetation, beaches and open spaces. But the central area around the bar, restaurant and aquarium pond is pleasant: neatly swept, attractive and shady under tall coconut palms. The large, curving beach has relatively course sand and the lagoon is terrribly shallow (the upside to this is that it is safe for children).

The bar is well stocked, the restaurant serves good food (all buffets), the staff are friendly and so are the other guests. For a well-priced diving or surfing holiday, close to the airport, this basic resort is now a strong contender.

Resort	*tel*: 440013	*fax*: 440012
	email: tari@tarivillage.com.mv	
can of beer: $3.30	half day-	
lime juice: $3.30	island hopping: $20	
mineral water: $3.30	sunset fishing: $10	
Dive centre	Albatros Top Diving	
	single dive, all equipment: $42	
	six dives, all equipment: $258	
	certified open water course: $420	

THUDUFUSHI

Flying.....25 mins
Speed boat.....n/a
Dhoni.....n/a

Ari Atoll, west

THUDUFUSHI IS MOSTLY ITALIAN DURING THE HIGH season and mostly British during the other seasons. All year round it is great value for money and a place that people love to come back to.

The resort is among a growing number of **all-inclusive** islands. But not every all-inclusive island is good value. On Thudufushi every aspect is of a high standard, and the fact that you don't have to worry about extra costs here and there is a real bonus.

Apart from whisky and champagne, all drinks are free. A selection of ten or so wines, including a fine Italian sparkling, are on offer with dinner. Included too is one picnic, one island hop and one sunset fishing. Snorkeling equipment, catamarans, windsurfers and canoes are free, so guests just pay for the motored sports: water-skiing and game fishing.

Free or not, all the equipment, like everything on the island, is in perfect condition. The level of maintenance and modernization is second to none and a resort that is eight years old looks like it opened last month. The game fishing boat is no conversion and the rods are made to the specifications of Franco Rosso and signed. The equipment in the dive school is the very latest.

Not so many people **dive** here, so the attention is personal and the diving is in small groups. Furthermore, there are only two other resorts in the whole central band of the atoll so the sites are always free. Two of the very best sites, Panettone and Thudufushi Thila, are right next door.

With the reef sweeping close around two

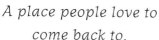

thirds of the island and coral running up near to the beach, the **snorkeling** is terrific. And the beach is just as good; broad and fine all the way around. Sadly, though, it has recently been felt necessary to build a lagoon wall, around about a fifth of the island.

A place people love to come back to.

Italian resorts generally have a high standard of **cuisine**, but Thudufushi is still a stand-out, particularly in the high season. The variety and quality of the food is surpassed by very few in the country. A dinner buffet may include such delicacies as octopus, duck, suckling pig, and smoked salmon.

It is difficult to find fault with Thudufushi, but some people may find the buildings a bit formal, even unsympathetic with their surroundings. This is not a place of thatch, whitewashed coral and sand on the floor. On the other hand, the people who love it here, love the free hairdressing salon, the free make-up salon and the chic boutique that share the reception building.

On top of all this, Thudufushi and its sister resort, Athuruga, are noticeably well-managed. It may be the difference between thinking of coming back and definitely coming back. And these two resorts have some of the highest return rates in the country.

Relative pric

6

8

Density of rooms to island size:

Resort	tel: 450597	fax: 450515
	email: thuadmin@dhivehinet.net.mv	

can of beer: $incl.	half day-
lime juice: $incl.	island hopping: $15
mineral water: $incl.	sunset fishing: $15

Dive centre	The Crab
	single dive, all equipment: $55
	six dives, all equipment: $300
	certified open water course: $480

THULHAGIRI

Flying.....n/a
Speed boat.....25 mins
Dhoni.....70 mins

North Malé Atoll

lagoon is generally very shallow, but small clumps of coral offer enough colourful fish to satisfy the snorkelling beginner.

The beach too is variable. Where there is a beach, it is massive, clean and fine-grained. And with a gently sloping, sandy-bottomed lagoon here it is almost perfect (there isn't much shade). Over a third of the island, however, has a wall after the sand and before the water. It is not unsightly as it is low, shapely and made of coral. Two small steps take you down to the water's edge.

〰 **THULHAGIRI IS A GOOD RESORT NOT FAR FROM THE** airport and the capital, Malé. It is a smart, handsome resort, but not imposing. The atmosphere is calm and casual, the environment is attractive and the staff are particularly friendly.

Although this is a small resort, it seems bigger because it is not rigidly laid out. There is a sandy path leading in from the jetty and the rest is up to you. You work out your own favourite way around the island. The rooms are not equally spaced all around the outside. And under the cover of many tall coconut palms, the place has more of a small village feel.

The centre of the village is the bar and lounge building, connected to the restaurant. The tall thatched roof sweeps low over open sides and a curving white wall. It is good looking but informal. With comfy chairs on a sandy floor and friendly bar staff it is a natural meeting place to while away the evenings or have a drink before meals.

The food is the pride of the resort. Clearly a lot of money is spent on the ingredients and the chefs. It is well known around that Thulhagiri puts on great buffets. And with three buffets a day you will have to pace yourself or do more of the exercise that's on offer. (Bed and breakfast and half board are offered as well as full board and even bed only.)

This is a pretty active resort. The watersports centre is well-equipped and well-used. Inside the atoll and with a near permanent cross wind it is particularly suitable for windsurfing lessons. Water-skiing, catamarans and banana boat are also available, with courses.

The dive school is a five star PADI Instructor Centre, well run and usually busy although it is quite small. The many dive sites in the south and east of the atoll are within easy reach. As for the island's own reef, it is variable. Parts of it are bare of corals but decent snorkelling is possible in other parts. And there are trips arranged to nearby reefs. The

The food is the pride of the place. It is well known around that Thulhagiri puts on good buffets.

The fifty eight rooms (all the same) are of a decent size and nicely decorated with batiks and thickly woven screw-pine matting. Each one has a/c, minibar and telephone. The fittings in the bathroom are good and the towels are fresh and soft. The shower is particularly good: modern and forceful, with an immediate supply of plentiful hot water.

Germans make up half the guests, the other half are a mix of Europeans, Australians and Japanese. Like the pet budgerigars that have multiplied all over the island, everyone seems to love it.

Resort	tel: 445930 fax: 445939
	email: reserve@thulaagiri.com.mv
can of beer: $3.63	half day- (speedboat)
lime juice: $3.85	island hopping: $95
mineral water: $3.85	sunset fishing: $18

Dive centre	Tropical Gangstars
	single dive, all equipment: $46
	six dives, all equipment: $276
	certified open water course: $420

Relative price:

8

9

Density of rooms to island size:

VADOO

Flying.....n/a
Speed boat.....20 mins
Dhoni.....55 mins

South Malé Atoll

perfectly placed to reach all the best sites in the southern part of North Malé Atoll, as well as the nearby sites, which are some of the best in South Malé. The one other top spot is around Guraidhoo, further south, and a day trip with lunch is regularly organised to dive it.

Of the fifteen designated Protected Marine Areas, five are within easy reach and two more (including Guraidhoo) are accessible. These areas are recognised as exceptional and in some way endangered, but some of the best diving in the country can be had within a few minutes

〜〜 VADOO IS A SMALL, EX-CLUSIVE RESORT, REBUILT IN the last year to the very highest stand-ards. It is a quiet, gentle place. At the same time, there are smiles all around and the atmosphere is warm and inviting. The tone is set by the Japanese guests,

who make up between a half and two thirds of the total. It is also set by the divers, as the same sort of percentage goes diving everyday.

Vadoo *Diving* Paradise is the full name, and it is not inaccurate. The island is

Relative price:

5

9

Density of rooms to island size:

of the resort. Old Shark Point and the Victory wreck in North Malé and Embudhoo Canyon and the Cathedral in South Malé are legendary.

Then there is the **house reef** itself. Just offshore is a steep wall. Moving north one passes a sandy bay of delicate coral and teeming reef fish. And at the northern edge morays, snapper and grouper play inside while sharks and trevally patrol the outside (in the Vadhoo Channel). Dolphins are often seen alongside the harbour jetty.

Partly because of the accent on diving, there is no organized evening entertainment, apart from a boat trip to Laguna Beach to go dancing. That is upon request, as are the other 'potential'

Small,

exclusive

and a

'Diver's

Paradise'

excursions, such as the Malé excursion, island hopping, local island visit, fishing and glass-bottomed boat. As a general rule the resort goes to bed early in preparation for the next day.

Or it could be because the **rooms** are so comfortable (or there are so

many honeymooners). There used to be three two-storey blocks, each with eight rooms. These have been demolished and rebuilt. Now there are two blocks and eight individual bungalows. Each room is decked out in marble and pine. No expense has been spared to bring the resort up to the top league. All the toilet fittings, for example, have been imported directly from Japan.

Despite the modern facilities every bungalow and block is roofed with thatch, to keep them in harmony with the environment. This is also true of the seven water bungalows (two of which are 'suites' with two bedrooms). These spacious, carpeted rooms have a glass table whose top comes off so you can feed the fish below, and private verandahs with steps down into the lagoon. And what a lagoon! At the bottom of the steps and out to the reef edge is a truly glorious **coral garden.**

There are two bars/lounges for relaxing during the day. One in the round over the water, to watch the sunrise and the sunset, and one brand new one built on

the beach, for the long easy evenings. The restaurant, too, has been completely rebuilt. The **food** is a mix of Japanese and Western, with local curries too.

This resort is undoubtedly in the top bracket. If you are not allergic to small places (it takes just six minutes to walk around), you are not looking to dance every night, and you are not 'euro-centric', you've got to love it here.

| Resort | tel: 443976 | fax: 443397 |
| email: vadoo@dhivehinet.net.mv | | |

can of beer: $3.75	half day-
lime juice: $3.28	island hopping: $18
mineral water: $4.12	sunset fishing: $24

Dive centre Vadoo
single dive, all equipment: $55
five dives, all equipment: $225
certified open water course: $525

VAKARUFALHI

Flying.....24 mins + 30 mins dhoni
Speed boat.....120 mins
Dhoni.....n/a

Ari Atoll, south-east

〰 **VAKARUFALHI IS A FINE LOOKING RESORT: SMALL,** round, with a perfect beach and reef encircling the island. Only opened a few years ago, all the buildings and facilities are as good as *new*. Comfort and beauty are assured, but it will take a while longer to develop a 'personality'.

The **beach** has suffered some erosion in one corner, so a low wall has been built in one part of the lagoon, but those are the only blemishes on an otherwise ideal setting. Much of the lagoon is shallow, clear and sandy, but the reef edge is not far away. So whether you fancy swimming and sunbathing or snorkelling the house reef, it is all on your doorstep. On the other hand, the windsurfers and catamarans can only be used in the lagoon at high tide. At other times they must be taken out into the open sea.

The **house reef** is very good for diving as well as snorkeling. Indeed the island is situated at the edge of the atoll's most popular channel for diving. Surprisingly, the **dive centre** is not heavily used; there are not always two boat dives a day. You can enjoy small group diving, but it may not be the best island for the seriously dedicated diver. Then again, it is ideally situated and this state of affairs is likely to change.

There are fifty **rooms,** all the same, though twelve are connected in pairs (family rooms) and thirty eight are individual bungalows. Each one is large and in 'as new' condition. The materials used are solid and good-looking. As well as a/c and hot fresh water there is a hairdryer and fridge (empty), but no telephone. The 'gifilli style' bathroom is attractive and well fitted. These are classy rooms topped off with thatched

Relative price:

6

7

Density of rooms to island size:

Sunbathing,

swimming and

snorkeling; it's on

your doorstep.

roofs that fit them comfortably into their environment.

The island is fortunate in having a large number of tall coconut palms. But in a few places it is somewhat scruffy as new plants take time to bed in and grow. Another small gripe is that the generator and desalination plants are a bit noisy in the middle of this small island.

The reception, bar and restaurant are all thatched and both well designed and decorated in the same natural shades of brown and coral. The large, round **restaurant** has a German chef who

prepares a good selection of buffets. Four evening meals are à la carte, one is set, one is a Maldivian buffet and one is a Western buffet. There is always plenty to eat, though occasionally the Italian guests ask for more Italian dishes.

Unusually, meal times are not full of laughter and conversation and the bar is quiet in the evenings. The island still seems to be trying to find the right mix of guests to make the place sparkle. At the moment it is not quite there. About half the guests are Germans and Swiss, while Italians make up a quarter and English another significant minority.

Vakarufalhi has all the natural assets of a classic coral island: nearby reef, wide beach and tall palms. On top of this, the buildings are well-made and well-decorated. In time it will also develop that elusive 'personality' that makes a place truly memorable.

Resort	*tel*: 450004	*fax*: 450007
email: vakaru@dhivehinet.net.mv		

can of beer: $3.50	half day-
lime juice: $2.50	island hopping: $15
mineral water: $2.50	sunset fishing: $10

Dive centre   Pro Divers
single dive, all equipment: $49
five dives, all equipment: $235
certified open water course: $548

VELAVARU

Flying....40 mins
Speed boat....n/a
Dhoni....n/a

Dhaalu Atoll

∿ REMOTE AND PEACEFUL, BEAUTIFULLY BUILT AND

sensitively managed. Add excellent food to the positive side and no housereef snorkeling to the down side and you have the essence of Velavaru.

Turtles (Velaa in Dhivehi) have long been associated with this island, and indeed many turtles were seen while constructing the resort. Most of them have gone now, but a plan is in place to help those that return to lay eggs. As a tribute, every roof on the resort is shaped like a turtle shell.

The most prominent turtle shell roof of all belongs to the dive base. There is no smarter dive centre building in the country. Ocean Pro run it admirably. Put your equipment in a basket and leave the rest to the team. As to the diving itself, it is biased towards the many local channels and tilas. The current can be strong, but then, the stronger the current the more likely you are to see the big fish. Sharks and rays are common and so too, encouragingly, are living corals. With just one other resort on the atoll (Vilu Reef), one resort to the north (Filitheyo) and none to the south, the dive sites are pretty much untouched.

Juerge, the dive base leader, said one day a blue marlin leapt out of the water right beside the dive dhoni. Maybe it knew that the management, although they run a big game boat, have a strict catch and return policy, and don't buy big game for the kitchens.

The housereef is too far to get to comfortably and anyway the coral emerges from the water at low tide and there are no channels cut through to the edge. To counter this drawback, there are two, free boat trips to one of three local spots, everyday.

The beach is very good, generally wide and soft, with the odd bit of erosion and sand pumping (which is less fine sand from the lagoon). Not every room has direct access to the beach, some are

Relative price

6

8

Density of
rooms to
island size:

tucked behind, but these are the last to be given out. In a rare move indeed, the management decided not to build all it had planned to, as it became clear that the island was filling up too much to maintain the atmosphere it wanted.

That atmosphere is one of peace and quiet, in comfort. There are no evening entertainments here. The tour rep. of the twenty percent or so of Italians organises separate events for them after dinner. (British make up around ten percent and Germans around two thirds).

The food is exceptional. Many resort buffets can be confidently predicted, but not these. Pan fried fish of course, but with shrimp butter sauce? Pasta with chickpeas, roulade of duck with orange sauce. Everyone is on full board.

There are eighty four rooms, of which eighteen are called superior, being slightly bigger and individual bungalows rather than semi-detached. They are round, handsome and well-finished. The look and feel is sunny and warm.

If you want to truly get away for a day, there's a lonely island a forty minute boat ride away, with bottomless white sand like talcum powder. But I bet you'll want to come back to Velavaru.

Resort	*tel*: 460028	*fax*: 460029
	email: info@velavaru.com.mv	

can of beer: $2.75	half day-
lime juice: $4.00	island hopping: $20
mineral water: $3.50	sunset fishing: $10

Dive centre — Ocean Pro
single dive, all equipment: $44
five dives, all equipment: $220
certified open water course: $480

VELIDHOO

〰 **VELIDHOO HAS BEEN MOVING UP-MARKET SINCE** the arrival of new owners and a new management team from Sri Lanka. It is only fair to say that there is still some way to go before it meets the high standards of most modern Maldivian resorts. The dive school, however, has always been, and remains, a very good reason to holiday here.

The island itself is a good size, not too big and not too small. But there are few palm trees or other plants and flowers. It is all oddly open to the skies. Most of the interior and areas behind the beaches could be called natural, they could also be called rough and unkempt. One walks around on a maze of paths that divide everywhere and disappear anywhere. It

could be that this is a welcome break from a too organised life at home. But there is no doubt cleaning up and sorting out needs to be done.

This applies to the **beaches** as well, which have old tumbled down groynes, poles, pipes and ropes across them. The south-west corner has a fine expanse of sand, but the west side has suffered bad erosion and the north side has both an outer wall and large groynes all the way down. The south side by the main jetty and outside the bar is good.

The **rooms** partly explain the haphazard layout of the island. First there were thirty bungalows, then another thirty were added, and then another twenty, making eighty in all. Some are near the

beach but many are tucked behind others. Some are close to each other, while some are more or less on their own. They are all solidly built in the round. Everything is in good order, though a comfortable chair would be nice. Twenty water bungalows are due to be built on the south side.

The dive school has always been a good reason to holiday here.

It is here that the best **snorkeling** is to be had. The reef then moves further off, but it is sufficiently good that the dive school organises boat trips to places on

Relative price

8

5

Density of
rooms to
island size:

the reef. Situated in the middle of the north section of the atoll, the sites east and west are accessible, as well as the hammerhead site on Rasdhoo Atoll.

The **dive centre** is run by friendly Germans who really put themselves out for their clients. The relaxed but professional atmosphere makes the diving experience enjoyable and safe.

The large, sheltered lagoon is particularly suited to **watersports**. Catamarans, canoes, windsurfers, water-skiing and parasailing are all offered here.

The reception, bar and restaurant area is different to the rest of the island. Here the garden is carefully planted and tended. The buildings are not quite grand, but not 'homey' either. There is much use of thick coir rope lashing wooden poles together - a cross between nautical neatness and desert island make-do. The bar is large, the music is loud and a platform spills out onto the beach where barbecues are held.

In the main restaurant the food is OK. Three quarters of the guests are on half board. There is a mix of set plates, buffets and 'specialist' buffets, like the beach barbecue and seafood nights.

Velidhu has always been a good place to do your diving. Now the resort itself is improving. It is not stylish and there is a way to go yet, but it's better than before.

Resort	tel: 450595 fax: 450630
	email: velidhu@dhivehinet.net.mv

can of beer: $2.50	half day-
lime juice: $4.40	island hopping: $20
mineral water: $2.75	sunset fishing: $18

Dive centre	Euro Divers
	single dive, all equipment: $51
	five dives, all equipment: $224
	certified open water course: $357+

VELIGANDU

Flying.....20 mins
Speed boat.....n/a
Dhoni.....n/a

Rasdhoo Atoll

ꝏON VELIGANDU YOU GET A LOT OF BEACH FOR YOUR

Not surprising when you discover that buck. Veligandu means *'sandbank'*.

The island's most unique feature is the long, L-shaped spit of sand that stretches out into the lagoon. A dream for serious tanners, it is permanently sunny and just a few metres from the water on either side.

As for the rest of the island the **beach** on the whole west side is getting bigger each year. Now it has stranded the two water bungalows on this side a good fifteen metres from the sea. Looking in the bright side, they are some of the only water bungalows in the country with their own stretch of beach!

On the east side, the beach is also very good, protected by large groynes. Indeed two of the four water bungalows here also step down onto sand. Opposite them in the water is a strip of outer wall.

Being essentially a sandbank the tree growth is not full or varied. The strength of the island is its atmosphere. It is one of those resorts where you feel able to kick off your shoes and do very little in a truly calm, *easy-going* environment. There is a young, responsive management team and the staff has remained almost the same since the resort opened fourteen years ago. This says a lot about the management, and is another why people come back here year after year.

There are sixty three **rooms** in three categories: superior (forty five), deluxe (eight) and water bungalows (ten). They are all essentially the same, with a few

Relative price:

8

9

Density of
rooms to
island size:

differences in size and detail. They are nothing really special, but all are light and airy, neat and tidy. The facilities are above average, with a full minibar, a hairdryer and telephone. Each has a 'gifili' bathroom and a large mirror.

used throughout the resort. Still, after a few days in a resort like this almost nothing can intrude on the sense of calm and relaxation that settles on you.

The **food** is very good. The number of different dishes in the buffets is not very high but the quality is all the better for that, and the Sri Lankan chef comes up with several interesting surprises (say, fishballs in yoghurt). An indication of the concern for guests' wishes is the three speciality brown breads made in the bakery each day from imported German flour.

The Swiss company Ocean Pro run the **dive** school, professionally and efficiently. There are a fair number of decent

dive sites around Rasdhoo Atoll, but the big prize here is the nearby - and unique in the Maldives - hammerhead shark point called Madivaru. Snorkeling on the house reef is OK. Not the best and not the worst.

A dream for serious tanners, it is always sunny and surrounded by water.

A guest relations officer ensures entertainments are well organised and plentiful in the evenings. It is a resort to relax, get a tan and have some fun. Out on Rasdhoo Atoll there is a real sense of being away from it all.

The reception, bar/coffee shop/dance floor/sundeck and restaurant are in one compact building decorated only in natural materials: thatch, wood, coral and weave on a sand floor (of course). One gripe is the candy-coloured painting scheme of pastel pink and blue that is

Resort	tel: 450594	fax: 450648
	email: veli@dhivehinet.net.mv	
can of beer: $3.10		full day-
lime juice: $5.70		island hopping: $14
mineral water: $2.63		sunset fishing: $11
Dive centre		Ocean Pro
		single dive, all equipment: $44
		six dives, all equipment: $264
		certified open water course: $480

VELIGANDU HURAA

Flying....n/a
Speed boat....45 mins
Dhoni....120 mins

South Malé Atoll

〰️**VELIGANDU HURAA IS THE SMALL, QUIET, CLASSY** resort of the three connected resorts that make up Palm Tree Islands. Dhigufinolhu is the young, active one and Bodu Huraa is the totally Italian one. A fourth connected island has all the noisy plant, such as the dive compressor and generators, so Veligandu is in the happy position of being exceptionally quiet and relaxing while still having access to all the daytime and evening entertainments on Dhigufinolhu, whenever desired. The price to pay for this convenience is views to the horizon interrupted by these resorts and the wooden walkways between.

Major renovations in late 2000 and an excellent new management team (the same as Dhigufinolhu) have improved an already very good resort. All the rooms have been entirely rebuilt. There are now eighteen deluxe rooms and five junior suites. They are all pleasantly decorated and have great showers. The suite rooms have a separate lounge area, a raised platform for the bed and an extra large bathroom. They also face south and are situated right on the beach. The deluxe rooms are shaded by low trees just a few steps away from the beach on the other side. A few large deluxe rooms are inside the island where it is even quieter and the view is to beautifully tended tropical flowers.

The gardening is indeed exceptional here. Narrow, white sandy paths move through a gorgeous array of flowers, shrubs and

bushes. Then in the very middle of the island is a superb stand of mature palm trees vaunting upwards. Underneath them is the main restaurant, al fresco.

Lunch is a three course menu, dinner is four course. Once a week there's a Maldivian buffet. The cuisine is of a high standard and set to go higher. If the day's menu is not to your taste, you can try the Asian specialty restaurant on the

Relative price:

6

4

Density of rooms to island size:

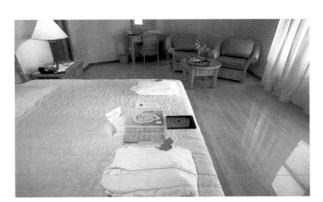

island or 'dinaround' at Dhigufinolhu's buffet or specialist grill restaurant. At five o'clock tea and cake is served in the bar/lounge, to the sounds of gentle jazz and light classics. Then you might linger to watch the sun go down and colour the sky behind Dhigufinolhu.

Snorkeling, unfortunately, is not an option near the island because the lagoon is so large and shallow but free snorkeling trips are put on to compensate for this and there's no charge for snorkeling equipment. Some dredging has taken place to create swimming pools by the beach. The pumped sand used to augment already good, wide beaches.

Diving hereabouts is excellent, with world class sites not far to the south. There are lots of opportunities to see the big fish as well as schools of the smaller fish and very encouraging coral regrowth.

The watersports, the excursions and entertainments are all organised out of Dhigu-finolhu. Veligandu Huraa guests can take it or leave it, it is all open to them. But, actually, the kind of guests that come here generally leave it. This is more a place for people who look forward to doing nothing but relaxing, being well fed and well looked after. A place where the only sounds are the waves and the birds.

Resort	tel: 443882	fax: 440009

email: dhigu@palmtree.com.mv

can of beer: $3.75	half day-
lime juice: $3.28	island hopping: $15
mineral water: $4.12	sunset fishing: $15

Dive centre Scuba Sub
single dive, all equipment: $65
six dives, all equipment: $312
certified open water course: $450

VILAMENDHOO

Flying........25 mins
Speed boat.......n/a
Dhoni........n/a

Ari Atoll, south-east

The resort also offers a greater variety of excursions than most: seven different resorts plus a number of inhabited and uninhabited local islands. A popular highlight is the local island of Dhangeti which has a cultural centre where visitors can see the old crafts in action, such as coir rope making, mat weaving and traditional cooking.

Around half the guests here are now all-inclusive, with the other half split evenly between half and full board. (Around half are English and half German, with a few Italians, French and Australians). All-inclusive means free drinking up to

*Some of the best snorkeling
to be had anywhere*

midnight (cocktails not included, but reasonably priced at $5), tea and snacks at 4-6, one free night fishing and one free island hop. It is now noticeable that there are more older people and children than before (more so in the high season).

The all-inclusive deal seems to suit everyone, except the dive school. And its true again here that the number of divers has gone down. It is also probable that the number of guests trying it out for the first time has increased. Certainly the quality of dive sites is still superb. This is the most renowned area for diving in Ari Atoll. Nearly all the dives are to tilas that start at least ten metres below the surface. As these tilas are deep down in fast flowing channels, not only are the big fish attracted, but many corals have survived the bleaching and many others started the recovery.

The housereef is also a good dive and snorkel, but the four cut-throughs and two jetties on the south side have had

∿ VILAMENDHOO IS ONE OF THE RESORTS THAT HAS

changed quite a bit in the last few years. It has moved away from the natural island with few facilities and lots of divers, to one that offers many facilities and particularly good value for money.

Facing west to the sunset and the large beach 'bulge', the beach bar doubles as a coffee shop and disco with pool table and gym included. Outside is a reasonable tennis court (plastic grass). Volleyball, table tennis, carom and darts are availabe too. Its all free, except $3 for the tennis equipment and $1.50 for a game of pool.

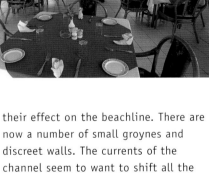

Relative price:

9

7

Density of
rooms to
island size:

their effect on the beachline. There are now a number of small groynes and discreet walls. The currents of the channel seem to want to shift all the sand to the tip of the island away from the open sea, that is, where the beach bar is. Happily facing west, so a great spot for sunset drinks.

The ten deluxe rooms are on the two tips of the island, around the rest of the island run the one hundred and thirty one superior rooms. Thirteen standard rooms are in the interior. Add to this a large service and cultivation area in the interior and sprawling public buildings and you have an island that is just about full up.

The buildings on the resort, particularly the beach bar/coffee shop, are not very attractive but the interiors of the rooms and reception have been upgraded with new furniture, including wooden loungers (instead of the old white plastic ones). More effort has been put into the cuisine too and the service, so all in all Vilamen-dhoo offers a good package at a very good price. Just those of us who remember the near pristine environment before...

Resort	tel: 450637	fax: 450639
	email: vilamndu@aaa.com.mv	

can of beer: $3.30	half day-
lime juice: $4.00	island hopping: $18
mineral water: $3.30	sunset fishing: $15

Dive centre   Vilamendhoo
single dive, all equipment: $50
six dives, all equipment: $284
certified open water course: $480

VILU REEF

Flying....40 mins
Speed boat....n/a
Dhoni....n/a

Dhaalu Atoll

〰️ OF ALL THE NEW RESORTS, VILU REEF HAS PERHAPS THE best natural assets. The concept and design is also good, but there are rather too many rooms squeezed onto the space and the build quality is not the best.

An ideal resort island geography is to have the house reef close-by on one side and the beach with sheltered lagoon on the other. Swaying palm trees across the island and leaning over the water's edge. That is how it is here, on the north-east tip of Dhaalu Atoll. It is not only close-by but the reef drops off into the atoll's most northerly channel. This means excellent diving and snorkelling, but it also carries a danger of strong currents sweeping into and out of the atoll. Aware

of this, the guest relations staff regularly check conditions and advise guests accordingly. Just snorkeling here could bring you face to face with dolphins, grey reef sharks or even a whale shark. As one of only two resorts on this new tourism atoll, the dive sites are fresh and 'fully stocked'.

The 'beach side' of the resort looks into the calm water of the lagoon. Ideal for watersports, the centre is larger and more active than most. The house reef side has beach as well, it is just not so wide and the corners suffer from a degree of erosion. The sand on the lagoon side is also wonderfully fine and deep. The jetty is on this side, next to the main bar and lounge. By happy coincidence this faces west, so the deck of the bar is the perfect place for a sundowner.

Coming off the jetty into the bar and lounge you see and feel the beautiful design concept. The roof is a swirling, thatched Nautilus shell, cowrie shells decorate the bar, shell-patterned textiles in muted turquoise green cover the

cushions of the low slung wicker chairs that are spread around the white sand floor. Excellent, and none of the other buildings quite live up to it.

The reception building is rather more functional. It has the shop, gymnasium, table tennis room and restaurant. The bar has the pool table ($5 an hour). In the centre of the island is a rough tennis court, an OK badminton court and a good volleyball court. Evenings are usually quiet, partly because most guests like it that way and partly because it's not easy bring down live acts all the way from Male'. Meals are all buffets; good but not exceptional, apart from having two Maldivian nights a week. Most people are on full board, about a third are half board and around ten percent, the British, are all-inclusive. A decent coffee shop is open twenty four hours a day.

The sixty-eight beach rooms look attractive: shell-shaped, with a good interior design that fits in a second bed and opens out to the beach. The walk-in clothes closet is an unusual and useful addition. Closer inspection turns up

Relative price:

6

10

Density of rooms to island size:

rather a lot of cheap, thin wood masquerading as quality. Built quickly, maintenance is already an issue. And you may not have a view of the beach. Most rooms are next to the beach, but a few are just behind the rooms that are just behind the beach front rooms. On top of this congestion, there are twenty-four garden rooms built inside the winding path that runs behind the beach rooms.

These rooms do not appear in the brochures.

German speakers make up two thirds of the guests, with British, Italians and French making up the other third, plus a few Japanese. Although the geography of the place is ideal, the build quality and, occasionally, the service, are weaknesses. The Maldivian owning company, however, has a reputation for integrity and

excellence so it should steadily improve.

Resort *tel*: 460011 *fax*: 460022
email: info@vilureef.com.mv

can of beer: $2.75   half day-
lime juice: $3.30   island hopping: $20
mineral water: $3.85   sunset fishing: $10

Dive centre   Dive Explorer
single dive, all equipment: $44
five dives, all equipment: $220
certified open water course: $480

VILLIVARU

Flying....n/a
Speed boat....60 mins
Dhoni....n/a

South Malé Atoll

VILLIVARU IS A SMALLER, QUIETER VERSION OF ITS sister island, Biyadoo. Like that island it has many fine palms, a good beach and a great location (as well as facilities) for diving. It is also 'child friendly'.

Although there is lush vegetation throughout the island, as with Biyadoo most of it is out of bounds for guests. They are restricted to either side of a path that goes around the outside only. On the other hand, all the rooms are set back ten to fifteen metres from the beach and in between is a lovely area of sand under the shade of tall palms. Hammocks are well placed around the island.

Because of this large area of shade, and because of the friendliness of the staff, parents and children feel comfortable here. (There are, though, no specific child

facilities such as baby-sitting). In general, guests tend to be a little older than average and the atmosphere is calmer.

Two extra beds will fit into the **rooms** for children and the management are happy to put them in. There are sixty rooms in six blocks of ten, with no difference between them. They are not particularly stylish inside or out, but the furniture is decent and the facilities are good. As well as a/c and h/c there is a minibar, hairdryer, tea/ coffee making facility and an electric mosquito repellent. Unlike Biyadoo, all the rooms are on the ground floor so one steps straight out onto the sand.

Every room has a good, sandy **beach** outside. The only area where the beach is not good is where the reception, restaurant and bar have sensibly been built. This area is the focus for the social evenings which

Relative price:

8

7

Density of rooms to island size:

go on quite late - making the mornings slow starters as well. Everyone is on *full board*. Breakfast and lunch are buffet, dinner is set. But for each dinner there is a choice of starter, and a main dish of meat, fish or chicken. There are also a number of speciality buffets. The chef, like the owners and managers, is Indian, and all the food is very tasty.

One of the best four or five dive regions in the resort atolls

The reef, varied in shape and topography, is accessible at several points around the island. With Biyadoo's reef also available for guests, *snorkelling* is popular and rewarding. *Diving*, too, is very popular, but it is not quite such a central aspect of this resort as it is in Biyadoo. Nonetheless, the centre is equally modern, spacious and well laid out.

Situated just inside the atoll from the famous channels around Guraidhoo and Kandooma, a large number of really top class dive sites are within a few minutes' dhoni ride from the island jetty. Excellent dive experiences are assured in what is surely one of the best four or five dive regions in all the resort atolls.

For all the qualities of the resort, the price of a holiday is very reasonable. So are the prices of the drinks. The same as Biyadoo's, it is all excellent value.

Resort	*tel*: 447070 *fax*: 447272
	email: resvn@biyadoo.com.mv

can of beer: $2.00	full day-
lime juice: $1.50	island hopping: $45
mineral water: $3.00	sunset fishing: $20

Dive centre	Jurgen Schaegger's
	single dive, all equipment: $47
	ten dives, all equipment: $440
	certified open water course: $462

Medhufushi

Flying....40 mins
Speed boat....n/a
Dhoni....n/a

Meemu Atoll

ᐯ ONE OF THE VERY LAST OF THE NEW RESORTS TO BE finished, Medhufushi looks like it will be worth the wait. Essentially simple in overall concept, it has real character and class.

The island is long and narrow, the rooms running the length of both sides. At one end is the service area, at the other, the water bungalows. Half way along is the whole public area, including the watersports and dive centres. In the lagoon at this point stands the main bar.

It's in a quiet section of the bar that you fill out the registration upon arrival. You don't go to the reception and you needn't ever know where it is. Requests and bookings can be made from your room, usually through one of the guest relations officers. It's a small indication of the thoughtful informality and level of service the management wish to provide.

In the same way, there's no lugging of dive equipment down the jetty on a hot afternoon. Just drop your equipment in a basket and the dive centre does the rest. As one of only two resorts in the atoll, the sites are pretty much untouched and, at this stage, mostly unknown as well. With just one nearby channel, very experienced Maldives' divers might not be satisfied, but combined with large overhanging giris, protected thilas, outside drift diving and a Manta point and cleaning station, there is plenty to keep everyone else happy.

Snorkeling, on the other hand, is the one disappointment of the resort. As with nearly all the new resorts, you can't swim to the reef edge, it's too far and, at low tide, it's too shallow, you have to wade out. At the end of the jetty the lagoon deepens, there are coral blocks and snorkeling is OK. Snorkeling trips will be a regular feature, to compensate.

The beaches are excellent: long, wide, white and uninterrupted, except for the one jetty. Only the slightest coarseness hints that it has been boosted by dredging.

With judicious pruning, the beach and the lagoon can be seen from each room, while leaving plenty of shade and greenery. On the whole it's an island with very good growth of mature palms. It will be a few years before the newly planted vegetation grows and thickens.

The rooms themselves are simple and elegant. A satellite tv and minibar are neatly hidden in a wooden cabinet in front of the four-poster bed. The room itself is not large, though the platform outside is generous and the half-open bathroom is a good size and attractively made. In addition to the beach villas there are family villas (two together) and a few beach villas suites. The water bungalows also come in three categories: regular, suites and honeymoon villas (two units out on their own in the lagoon).

The key difference between the rooms is whether they have the morning sun or the afternoon sun. This is particularly important for the residents of the water bungalows who can't walk over to the other side.

They can, however, stroll down to the pool which faces West, just at the water's edge. Or take a seat in one of the lounges of the beautiful main bar and watch the sun set with drink in hand.

The food should be at least as good as it is in Medhufushi's sister island, Filitheyo and that is very good.

Resort	tel: 324933	fax: 324943
	email: sale@aaa.com.mv	
can of beer: $2.00		full day-
lime juice: $1.50		island hopping: $45
mineral water: $3.00		sunset fishing: $20
Dive centre		Werner Lau
	single dive, all equipment: $47	
	ten dives, all equipment: $440	
	certified open water course: $462	

ROYAL ISLAND

Flying....30 mins
Speed boat....n/a
Dhoni....n/a

Baa Atoll

ROYAL ISLAND IS VILLA HOTELS' FIFTH RESORT -
the others are Sun, Fun, Holiday and Paradise - and it is intended to be the jewel in the crown. It has been a long time in the making - and was still a few months off opening when I visited - partly because the standards set, in just about every aspect of construction, are second to none in the whole country. Whether the guest sees it or not everything used to make this resort is the best available.

I can't yet judge the cuisine but it has every chance of being first rate as the kitchen is amazing, matched only by that on Kanuhuraa.

The swimming pool will be a spectacular showpiece of curves, slopes and countless tiny blue tiles. The jacuzi, in the spa, is in the same recoco style.

No expense has been spared. There is a single indoor badminton court in a building that will last a hundred years. So too the squash court. The tennis court and basketball courts are built to international standards. The dive centre and watersports centre will be as well stocked as any resort in the country.

The resort has one hundred and fifty rooms. One hundred and forty eight deluxe and two presidential suites. The furniture is solid hardwood, the marble on the bedside tables is real, heavy marble. The curtains, bedcovers and cushion materials are rich and expensive and look it. The bathroom fittings are the best you can find.

By now I'm sure you get the picture. Either this is just what you are looking for or it is just what you are not looking for. This is a resort that will truly satisfy the lust for luxury and first class facilities. Many of us have that longing, but in the context of a

lonely Maldivian island... well, it's really not that appropriate. The contrast between the regal, heavy interiors and the spare, simple nature outside is quite startling.

It's a fine island in itself. The many buildings have had to find space for themselves, but the tall palms have been kept intact throughout. The real glory of the nature here, though, is the number of outstanding banyan trees. These beautiful monsters do give a special feeling to the interior. They were apparently planted several hundred years ago, when the island was last inhabited, to provide ready-made boat masts.

One of the last inhabitants of the island is said to have been the great Maldivian hero Bodu Thakarufaanu's mother. The bathing pool she would have used is still preserved.

In its original state the beaches were narrow and uncertain but now, after shifting over nearby sandbanks, they are wide and set in place.

The snorkeling should be good as the reefs are very close by all around this cigar-shaped island in the channel.

Going by the other Villa hotels, the service and guest relations should be excellent. It really all comes down to a matter of taste.

Resort	tel:	fax:
	email:	
can of beer: $		full day-
lime juice: $		island hopping: $
mineral water: $		sunset fishing: $
Dive centre		
	single dive, all equipment: $	
	ten dives, all equipment: $	
	certified open water course: $	

When you come back to Male' **Kaimoo** You'll want to come back to us

It may be the warmth of our welcome, the style of our service or the comfort of our rooms. It may simply be our proximity to the jetty but whatever it is, once you've stayed a night with us you won't look around anymore.

For the budget conscious Kai Lodge is the place. For the up-market visitor Kam Hotel can't be beaten. And for the longer stay, our luxurious apartments provide all you could wish for.

Call 322212   Fax 318057   email kaimoo@dhivehinet.net.mv

During your visit to Maldives don't forget to visit

SOUVENIRS

Come up to Souvenirs
and be surprised

Above the noise of the street take your time to browse around the largest collection of holiday goods in the country.

With twelve years experience in this business, we have a feel for what you like and we go out of our way to get it for you. Almost everything in our shop is original work commissioned by us with you in mind. With t-shirts ranging from $3 to $45, batiks of every description, sarongs of every material, jewelry of precious

stone and silver, wood carvings, teas, spices and so much more, we're a one-stop holiday shop.

So don't be sidetracked, come upstairs and be delighted.

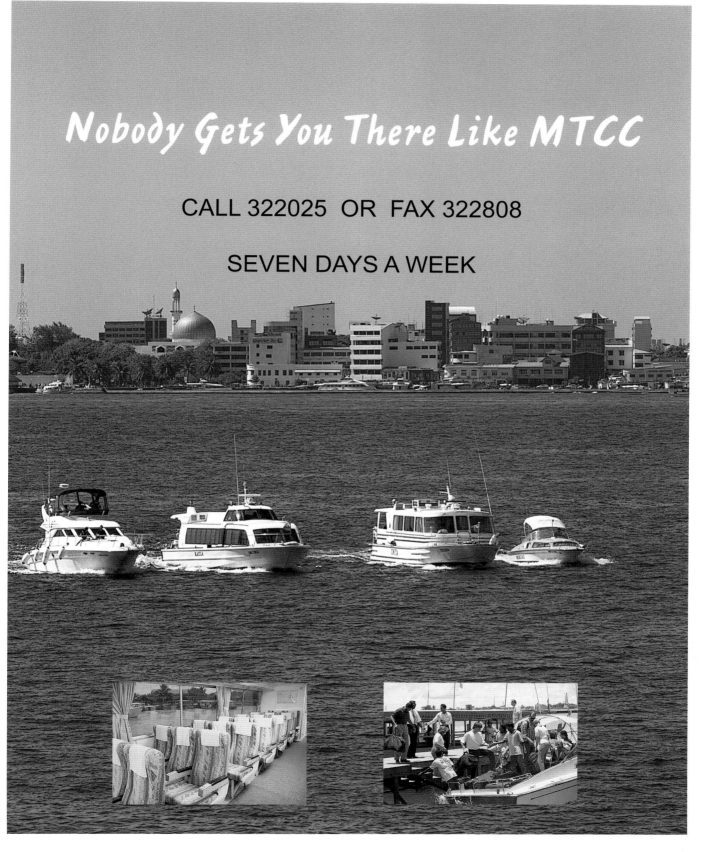

Nobody Gets You There Like MTCC

CALL 322025 OR FAX 322808

SEVEN DAYS A WEEK